the
ultimate
film
guides

# GoodFellas

### Director
## Martin Scorsese

Note by Iain Colley

Longman        Y York Press

For Scott and Mazza, with my love

York Press
322 Old Brompton Road, London SW5 9JH

Pearson Education Limited
Edinburgh Gate, Harlow, Essex CM20 2JE, United Kingdom
Associated companies, branches and representatives throughout
the world

First published 2001

ISBN 0-582-45250-3

Designed by Vicki Pacey
Phototypeset by Gem Graphics, Trenance, Mawgan Porth, Cornwall
Colour reproduction and film output by Spectrum Colour
Produced by Addison Wesley Longman China Limited, Hong Kong

# contents

What is honour? A word.
What is that word, honour? Air.

*Shakespeare*

There are several million
inhabitants of New York. Not
all of them eke out a precarious
livelihood by murdering one
another, but there is a definite
section of the population which
murders – not casually, on the
spur of the moment, but on
definitely commercial lines.

*P.G. Wodehouse*

Film is like a battleground: love,
hate, action, violence, death.
In one word: EMOTION.

*Samuel Fuller*

**author of this note**  Dr Iain Colley is a freelance writer and lecturer based in Lancaster. His fiction, verse and critical writing have appeared in a variety of publications, and he has authored *Easy Rider* for the York Film Notes series.

# background

# trailer

Gangster films are exciting. They make a spectacle out of lawbreaking. The gangster may be doomed – punished by death or imprisonment for his transgression – but he lives high, fast and hard before Nemesis overtakes him. The romance of the gangster is founded on the perception that the bad guys can be more fascinating than virtuous, clean-cut heroes. The gangster is a dissident who breaks the rules. He may also, as Paul Kooistra argues, appeal to an alternative sense of justice.

The gangster movie genre, as it has evolved, is primarily American. Organised crime may be global, and plenty of gangster films are made elsewhere in the world, but America has stamped its own likeness on the **iconography** of the genre. Over seventy years the generic locations have expanded from Chicago, LA and New York to include more recent crime nuclei such as Las Vegas, Miami and Detroit, but the neon-lit streets of American cities remain the cultural habitat of the gangster. And the style of the gangster – hyperactive, showy and overbearing – is also American.

The gangster picture emerged – unlike the Western – from a fully contemporary American reality (see Contexts: Genre). While it's widely accepted that the gangster continues some of the traditions of the old Western hero, he is, as Robert Warshow notes 'the man of the city', not of the wide open spaces. He readily stands for the national archetype of a driven, purposeful energy that is liable to overreach or spiral out of control: the No, as Warshow sees him, to the great American Yes. By being 'anti', the gangster has achieved the status of a salient mythic figure in the pantheon of popular culture.

*GoodFellas* is an example of a gangster movie that draws on a rich repertoire of cinematic elements. It is both a generic, mass-audience picture and a film by a respected auteur with a vision of 'personal' cinema. A specimen of the 'male action genre', it also incorporates the voice and the perspective of a mob wife. It expressly claims to be 'based on a true story', yet it's powerfully inventive. It incorporates the finely crafted professionalism of the old studio system, in the products of which Scorsese had immersed himself; at the same time it liberally employs what he has called 'all the tricks of the New Wave'.

The film holds these elements together, but it tells a story of disintegration as radical conflicts pile up for the wiseguys: between group loyalty and the individualist ethic; between Italian custom and American sovereignty; between their two 'families'; and between the insecure halves of their split identities. The result is a movie that in ten years has become widely accepted as a classic.

Most people who see *GoodFellas* will have no direct knowledge of the world it represents; at the same time it will be immensely familiar to many of them. Italian-American gangsters; daring heists; outbursts of deadly violence; rivalry and double-crossing within the gang: the grossly indulgent pleasures of the affluent mobster–Hollywood cinema, television and the print media have made all these familiar.

*GoodFellas* derives from Nicholas Pileggi's source book *Wiseguy* (see Contexts: Source Book/True Crime), which belongs to the subgenre of true crime in which the story is told from within the mob by a defector, adding a spicy authenticity. By true-crime standards *Wiseguy* is a sober account which doesn't excuse or heroicise Henry Hill. But where gangster stories are concerned, just to tell the story is to enter the realm of myth.

Gangsters are endlessly processed into myth at the same time as gangster chronicles lay claim to 'truth' and 'realism'. Anyone viewing *GoodFellas* is watching a highly mediated story – a fiction. Yet there are real-world gangsters, including highly active and powerful (and international) networks of organised crime. No one doubts that they rob and murder, traffic in drugs and carry out other 'victimless' crimes, and launder money through respectable fronts. Gangster films are not science fiction or fantasy. Whatever their approach or viewpoint, they address a social reality (see Style: Realism). Understanding *GoodFellas* means adopting a dual perspective, on the role of gangsters in American society and on the workings of Hollywood cinema. Both organised crime

a horrifying, unblinkered view of humanity

and the studio system enjoyed rapid industrial growth in the 1920s. They have been bedmates ever since.

Film reviews are not infallible measures of either artistic or commercial success, but they are an integral part of the complex processes that accompany a film release. They range from the nakedly promotional to the near-academic, and they are, in the end, opinion. But the standards, explicit or not, by which they appraise new movies offer clues to the prevailing taste in films, and therefore to the critical ideologies reflected in reviewers' judgements. Most reviews of *GoodFellas* were admiring and positive.

Desson Howe, *Washington Post* (21 September, 1990) decided that

> Scorsese seems to have gone for broke. But 'GoodFellas' ... is not just a feature-length random killing spree. It's an unleashing of his talents. There's a gutsy passion there, as well as a horrifying, unblinking view of humanity. Artistically at least, Scorsese has managed to make crime pay.

'Humanity' here seems to stand for the bonds of fellow-feeling an audience is invited to share with flawed or transgressive characters. Roger Ebert of *Chicago Sun-Times* wrote

> most films, even great ones, evaporate like mist once you've returned to the real world; they leave memories behind, but their reality fades fairly quickly. Not this film, which shows America's finest filmmaker at the peak of his form. No finer film has ever been made about organized crime.

Ebert saw the movie's central theme as guilt and related it to Scorsese's Catholic upbringing, a common critical analysis of Scorsese's work. *Variety* found *GoodFellas*

> colorful but dramatically unsatisfying, ... the second half doesn't ... develop the dramatic conflicts between character and milieu that are hinted at earlier.

'a movie so surefooted'

*Variety*'s reviewer, like several others, may have found the big-name De Niro under-used.

Kathleen Murphy of *Film Comment* (September-October 1990) found *GoodFellas*

> a movie so surefooted, so teeming with authentic action, color, character and risk it literally takes your breath away.

In the UK Tom Milne, *Monthly Film Bulletin*, praised it as

> superbly shot ... a fascinating, intelligent and in some ways ground-breaking movie.

By 1990, despite some box-office failures, Scorsese was an established director who was expected to deliver. A new film by him was an event, even if he never made the family-oriented sagas and action blockbusters that earned the huge grosses. His success had created expectations, and he was returning to the kind of urban subworld where he had first earned success.

# reading goodfellas

From its early days, the crime picture made the authorities nervous. If screen stars were role-models, would audiences be tempted to emulate the **charismatic** hoodlum rather than the clean-cut saviour-rescuer hero? Such fears led to the issuing of didactic warnings. A foretitle added to *Little Caesar* (1930) and *Public Enemy* (1931) deplores 'the evils associated with prohibition' and urges the public to cooperate in solving them. This high-minded appeal to responsible citizenship – 'good government bullshit', in Henry Hill's words – prefaced a narrative that climaxed in the mobster's ruin and destruction.

Such moral cautions now seem mealy-mouthed and condescending. But they amounted to a recognition that the crime film, if it was not to be bland and evasive, was by the nature of its material potentially subversive. It was bound to push at the frontiers of acceptable taste and attract the concern of censors. While in **classic Hollywood** a genre like

theft, hijacking, intimidation, murder

romantic comedy skirted issues such as premarital sex and adultery on tiptoe, the gangster picture directly confronted theft, hijacking, intimidation and murder. The nervousness of the official response was a tacit acknowledgement of its vitality.

The gangster is supposedly the public enemy, not a public benefactor like the archetypal Western hero, whose task is to make himself redundant fighting to establish law and order. The gangster is the dark urban *alter ego* of the Western saviour, undoing the work of the law. While the Western hero sacrifices himself for the sake of the future, the gangster lives selfishly in the moment, till his misdeeds catch up with him, when typically another mobster takes his place. The gangster can't be an unambiguous hero, though he commonly attracts populist sympathy and admiration, which the cautionary epigraphs sought to allay.

However, the modern gangster film doesn't usually attempt to enforce any clear-cut moral lessons. There is much more emphasis on the 'family' structure of organised crime, its internal relations and politics, and its liaisons with legitimate business and politics. You could perhaps infer from Henry Hill's story that, though crime may pay, it doesn't pay for ever. He runs into the dead-end logic of his chosen career path. Henry, unlike earlier incarnations of the gangster, doesn't die. Instead he's reduced and humiliated, becoming a protected government informer and a 'schnook' as he is squeezed between bleak alternatives. There is no doubt that he has chosen his fate – what goes around, comes around.

Yet *GoodFellas* has little time for a real-world moral debate about crime and punishment. It's far more about what an audience *feels* as *GoodFellas* uses the screen space to envelop it in the values and attitudes of the wiseguys as they go about their crooked business. Glimpses of 'normal' society are marginal, intermittent and hardly affirmative. Henry's jaundiced father beats him, the nice boy across the street is an aggressive groper, cops take bribes as a matter of course, the cordial face of the leisure industries conceals mob rule. The view is from within the criminal half-world. At the same time the criminal milieu, though clannish, is implicated in the wider world, not quarantined from it.

The film starts *in medias res* (see Narrative & Form: Narrative in

a grisly panic that has its comic side

GoodFellas) and in the past. The opening captions in plain white text zip off the screen to the sound of car tyres and engines. The first of them announces that 'This film is based on a true story'. Place and time are added: 'New York, 1970'. The printed words are minimal and neutral. The active interest is in the visuals.

What the screen first reveals is a grisly panic that also has its comic side, though not for Henry. The first view of him does not show a confident, hardened criminal. At the wheel of the coupé taking Billy Batts's body for furtive burial, foreground right as the visual centre of attention, he looks anxious. His harshly lit face is weary and strained. His sense of urgency isn't shared by Jimmy, who is sleeping in the front passenger seat, or Tommy in the unlit rear of the car. When the knocking in the trunk forces Henry to pull up, the three men stand well clear in the infernal glare of the rear lights (redolent of the red-lit bar in *Mean Streets*, where the pleasures of hanging out are chronically invaded by anger and tension).

It's left to Henry to unfasten the trunk. As the lid rises, it reveals that Billy, a bloody mess wrapped in tablecloths, is hopelessly beyond any kind of retaliation; nonetheless Tommy and Jimmy, who have kept guardedly back, react as though he is a threatening, unkillable monster. Tommy, cursing, stabs him frenziedly. Then Jimmy fires four bullets from his revolver into the body.

Henry takes no part in this grisly assault. He stands apart, immobile and blank, until, isolated in the frame, he steps forward to close the trunk. As he does so his retrospective voice-over is heard saying: 'As far back as I can remember I always wanted to be a gangster'. The frame freezes on his haunted expression, head tilted up as if to contemplate some troubling destiny, and at this point 'Rags to Riches' is heard on the soundtrack (see Style: Music), while the movie's title appears on a dark screen, this time in blood-red capitals.

This opening sequence is presented with Scorsese's typical narrative speed and economy. Though the characters are not instantly identified, the situation wouldn't puzzle an audience who knows the genre: gangsters kill people and dump their bodies in remote places. Yet here the operation is not smoothly efficient. The supposed corpse isn't dead,

an icy stone killer like Jimmy

and the jumpy response foreshadows *GoodFellas*' representation of organised crime as clumsy and anarchic, unlike the well-ordered corporate hierarchy of the Mafia family in *The Godfather.*

Henry appears as the subordinate member of the trio, performing the menial tasks, and also as the nonviolent one. Tommy and Jimmy had initially battered Billy (as is later shown), and they finish him off. But as a passive accomplice Henry shares the guilt, and his features show it even as his words of naïve infatuation with the gangster lifestyle are heard on the soundtrack. Is *this* brutal and horrific scene what he wanted? What has been shown so far suggests that he's neither a short-fuse flake like Tommy nor an icy stone killer like Jimmy.

The opening sequence establishes Henry as a foreground figure and raises ironic questions about his choice of occupation. His fear is evident and well founded. This is a world in which men are routinely murdered, where there are no rules of evidence and no court of appeal, where – as the voice-over presently explains – 'what Paulie and the organisation does is offer protection for people who can't go to the cops ... That's all it is. They're like the cops for the wiseguys.'

But that's *not* all it is. Organised crime may be a contorted mirror-image of civil society, but for that reason it shares its contradictions. The play-off between personal survival and group loyalty is intensified where there is no properly regulated system of justice. 'Protection' not only costs money. It's partial and limited. It can easily turn into bullying or assassination. Crime attracts damaged, erratic personalities. It's not the province of the 'ordinary schnook'. It's more glamorous and exciting – as Henry sees it – but far riskier. And, in the end, even those who enjoy the risk don't want to pay the price; there's little honour among thieves.

*GoodFellas*' representation of criminal business practice closely matches Robert Lacey's description of it in *Little Man*:

> Criminals, high and low, are risk takers and deal makers – and fairly short-term deal makers at that ....
>
> Criminal life is ... a succession of deals. The average modern wiseguy has, typically, four or five deals in the air at any one

united by their dishonesty and violence

> time. They are partnerships, in varying combinations, that he has
> put together with his own immediate contacts, with the
> members of other criminal rings, and from time to time, with a
> recruit from the straight world .... It is a matter of individual
> enterprise, and the share-out at the end of it ... is the measure of
> how successful any particular deal has been.

In *GoodFellas* there is no criminal super-corporation, no grand military structure with its graded ranks and exact specialisms. Italian-Americans of Sicilian descent have a privileged place in it, but no giant Mafia octopus overshadows and regulates a vast criminal empire. In fact, the emphasis is on the localisation of crime, the proximity of Idlewild Airport offering a convenient cash-cow. These are East New York gangsters from 'the boroughs', patrolling and operating in a limited, known territory, and it is on Henry 's out-of-state mission to Florida that he is heavily busted.

*GoodFellas* therefore also confronts the popular idea of a traditional community with that of a counter-community, an urban underworld whose members are united by their dishonesty and violence, qualities that deny the communitarian ideal of mutual aid and common allegiances. On the cultural level, Henry, Paulie, Jimmy and Tommy share many tastes and interests with affluent blue-collar or middle-class American men. They like the 'carpet joints', the night spots, the girls, the clothes and jewellery, the leisure drugs (see Contexts: Lifestyle & Consumerism). They pay tribute to broadly conservative 'family values'. But they live under self-created pressures that constantly threaten to collapse their unity. This paradox, which the FBI exploits against the wiseguys, drives the plot.

Henry is an active player in the dynamics of gangster enterprise, a man who lives to make deals, some of them spectacular. This propels him into the networks of male association that some of Scorsese's best work studies. It's a parallel world to that of the 'citizen'. The rules are shifting and uncertain and the sanctified American credo of success and self-improvement fuels conspiracy, plunder and death. *GoodFellas* aims to make the audience feel what a world is like where a small mistake can get you 'whacked out'.

generally cast as an anti-hero

# key players' biographies

## ROBERT DE NIRO

De Niro dominates the posters and other graphic publicity (book covers, etc.) for *GoodFellas*. Foreground centre in the group photo, he stares directly ahead with an expression on his strong, shadowed features that is dangerous but slightly jaded and hollow – always in character.

De Niro is conclusively the star as serious screen actor. The son of artists, he pours a studied intensity into his work. In many respects he invites comparison with Marlon Brando, but De Niro lacks Brando's wasteful contempt for his craft, and his fierce professional discipline has been apparent in his management of his body shape – notably in *Raging Bull* and *Cape Fear*.

Though they have not always worked together, De Niro and Scorsese are an accomplished partnership, with De Niro generally cast as anti-hero, and for most filmgoers one name automatically invokes the other. De Niro appeared losing it as Johnny Boy in *Mean Streets* (1973), losing it even more as Travis Bickle in *Taxi Driver* (1975), and as Jimmy Doyle, not getting the girl, in *New York, New York* (1977) – De Niro's parts seem to merge the two classic ethnic types in Hollywood gangster films, Irish and Italian. In *Raging Bull* (1980) he gave an unforgettable performance of macho masculinity in breakdown. As *The King of Comedy* (1988) he played the fan from hell in a surgical satire on the cult of fame. After *GoodFellas* he hammed his way through the mediocre *Cape Fear* (1991) to a watery death, but in Scorsese's masterpiece *Casino* (1995) he was commanding as the Las Vegas gambling boss.

De Niro has played few conventional romantic or action heroes, though he has often played figures with a definite renown or notoriety, whose ego-satisfaction chronically depends on the effect they have on others. Travis Bickle, Jake La Motta, Rupert Pupkin, all become famous by compromised, vicious or fraudulent means: the means scarcely matter to them, any more than they do to the gangster.

veering ... between bonhomie and ballistic rage

## RAY LIOTTA

Probably many filmgoers' first impression of Ray Liotta was his appearance as the spectral Shoeless Joe Jackson in *Field of Dreams* (1989), a magical reappraisal of the 1960s in the guise of a baseball fantasy. The role called for an actor who could appear likeable and sensitive, even innocent, despite a proven taint of corruption, and – because the character was an athlete – possessed physical grace and strength. Against the blandness of the leading man, Kevin Costner, Liotta was distinctive. Along with boyishly handsome features he had the restraint of pose and gesture proper to an apparition.

The blend of personal attractiveness and a latent dark side in its protagonists is a long-standing device of the gangster film. It has erotic implications, and may also hint that the criminal is potentially good, whatever his choices or his conditioning have made him – that he could have become the priest rather than the wiseguy. Liotta's casting does not ask the audience to condone Henry's criminality, but he has a winning male prettiness with a touch of the roughneck, rather after the fashion of Tony Curtis. It aids his dramatic function as a focus of empathy. It also explains Karen's attraction.

## JOE PESCI

Joe Pesci made his first appearance as an extra in *Hey, Let's Twist* (1961), but was only in regular film work after his role in *Raging Bull*. He won a Best Supporting Actor Oscar for *GoodFellas*, playing a role that harked back to traditional psychopathic furies like Tommy Powers and Rico Bandello. He was effectively to reprise the part in *Casino*, veering unpredictably between bonhomie and ballistic rage. Short and stocky like Edward G. Robinson, Pesci is an example of the kind of gifted actor Hollywood often uses in character roles. Pesci does indeed look like a funny man, a clown, not an all-American hero, and the by-play with Henry over his talents as a raconteur – 'What's so funny about me?' – underlines this (see Style: Dialogue). It also tells the audience that Tommy is a walking time-bomb, and the psycho role tends to stick to Pesci.

cold eyes and an aggressive mouth

## PAUL SORVINO

Paul Sorvino, a native New Yorker and an opera singer, plays the boss in the background, a neighbourhood *capo*, and when the group photo is doctored to fit a narrow format he is the one left out. Sorvino has the looks for the part of a powerful boss – heavy-jowled, with cold eyes and an aggressive mouth. His career in television and movies since the early 1970s has also included many police roles as well as other mature authority figures such as priests and doctors. 'Authority' in gangster cinema can be signified equally by the cop, the hoodlum and the priest; it calls for actors of the same physical type.

## LORRAINE BRACCO

Lorraine Bracco, once a Jean-Paul Gaultier model, divides the voice-over with Henry and plays Karen as much more than a moll. In a supporting role which earned her an Oscar nomination, she plays a feisty and assertive woman whose expectations of marriage and family life are ruined by Henry's involvement with the mob. Bracco began her acting career in Europe, where she modelled, and had played relatively few American cinema and television parts before *GoodFellas*, though her role in *Someone To Watch Over Me* (1987) raised her career profile. Since *GoodFellas* she has impressed as Jennifer Melfi, Tony Soprano's therapist in the fine television Mafia series *The Sopranos*. Her voice modulated to a robotic clinical whisper that betrays Jennifer's own tensions, she confronts the neurotic hoodlum Tony Soprano with the image of the educated, achieving woman.

De Niro, Sorvino and Bracco are all native New Yorkers, Liotta and Pesci were born just across the Hudson River in Newark, New Jersey. All have Italian surnames, like the director. Playing scenes with the intuitive understanding of an acting ensemble, getting the inflections and the gestures right, they epitomise the wide talent pool of American screen acting.

## MARTIN SCORSESE

Martin Scorsese was a 'war baby', born in 1942 in Flushing, Long Island but living from the age of seven or eight on Manhattan's Lower East

a disregard for social structures

Side – 'Little Italy'. The biographical foundations for his career as a director are well known and Scorsese is quite interview-friendly. He records that 'Little Italy was very sharply defined, so often the people from one block wouldn't hang out with those from another .... We didn't care about the Government, or politicians or the police; we felt we were right in our ways'. This mixture of narrow, conservative 'ways' and a disregard for the official structures of American society equates with the outlook of the gangster group – subversive in its illegal practices, but far from politically radical.

Passionate about cinema like many of his generation, Scorsese chose to study film at New York University, where he later taught. This makes him one of the first generation of directors (the 'movie brats') to come up through the film schools; earlier ones had got into the business somehow, even as extras, then learned their trade and built their careers within the **studio system**. By the end of the 1960s he had made three short films and a feature (*Who's That Knocking At My Door?*) which suffered delayed distribution and title changes. In 1970 he was an editor on *Woodstock* and also directed the documentary *Street Scenes 1970*, covering student demonstrations to protest against Nixon's bombing of Cambodia. Two years later he directed a cops-and-robbers story with a radical edge produced by Roger Corman for American International Pictures, *Boxcar Bertha*, described by *Time Out* as 'superior formula stuff, injected with a rare degree of life by enthusiastic direction'.

Scorsese's graduation from NYU hadn't given him a meal-ticket as a director, but Corman was a generous talent spotter. He loved to hire new faces with fresh ideas to work on the low-budget shockers that became a cult for young moviegoers. In Scorsese's words: 'The best post-graduate training you could get in America at that time was to work for Roger Corman.'

The 1970s established Scorsese, first as a promising newcomer, then as an accomplished master. *Mean Streets* (1973) epitomised a New Hollywood cinema, examining the rituals and transactions of a subcultural corner of Manhattan through European-influenced and **cinema vérité** techniques; a potent use of popular music magnified its drive and vigour. It was followed by *Alice Doesn't Live Here Any More* (1974), *Taxi Driver* (1975) and *New York, New York* (1977). A marvellous documentary on The Band, *The Last Waltz*, with Scorsese as Socratic interviewer, appeared in 1978. *Raging Bull* (1980) almost instantly entered the critics' list of modern classics, though it disappointed the box office.

The next decade proved Scorsese's ambition, his versatility and to some extent his inconsistency, as his vision of a personal cinema collided with institutional and financial realities and the celebrity lifestyle kicked in. *The King Of Comedy* (1982) was an unhappy experience for the director, though it provided a fine role for De Niro, and for audiences a Jerry Lewis picture at last worth going to see. Unfortunately, too few did. *After Hours* (1985) was an intriguing venture into **existential** territory. But *The Color Of Money* (1986) was a dull sequel to *The Hustler*, as the later *Cape Fear* (1991) was a lumbering remake of a film in which Robert Mitchum's sleepy subtlety of expression exuded more menace than De Niro's beefcake monster (both made money).

The *Last Temptation Of Christ* was a serious religious movie probing the tensions of Christ's human-divine nature, but, despite the angry polemics it aroused, one of limited appeal. Scorsese's other projects during this time included pop promos and an Armani commercial, plus one episode of a television series and a forty-four-minute contribution to the compilation film *New York Stories* (1989), in which the other directors were Woody Allen and Francis Coppola. Scorsese's segment, *Life Lessons*, is a wry short story of a film, sending up the artistic ego.

In some sense, then, *GoodFellas* is a comeback movie as well a preparation for the 1995 gangster masterpiece *Casino*. But in its own right it is a film that plays to Scorsese's strengths as a film artist. It marries a personal imagination to the strengths of a firmly planted popular genre. It has a brilliant eye for 'the bits in between', the loose, untidy edges of life, the symptomatic details that have always caught the attention of the great realists (see Style: Realism). It explores the tortured myths of masculine strength, prowess and loyalty. It both relays

authorship is not an absolute

the insider-feel of a subculture, and makes the subcultural group a means of anatomising American society in its movement through three decades.

# the director as auteur

The notion of authorship is problematic. As a way of finding serious **aesthetic** value in the products of an industrialised mode of production – 'Hollywood' – it boosted Film Studies in the 1960s and 1970s by hijacking high-cultural criteria, above all the role of the single creative individual. The French term **auteurisme** was adopted and developed as 'authorship theory' in England and the United States, largely as a rationale for the serious study of popular film. Auteurisme – a committed approach rather than a strict theory – became a way of canonising directors (Hawks, Hitchcock, Ford, Welles, etc.) who were held to have 'transcended' the institutional constraints of the studio system. Later theoretical developments challenged this cornerstone idea, substituting the more impersonal critical apparatus of structuralism, semiotics and psychoanalysis.

Authorship is not an absolute. Especially in a collaborative art like cinema, it is never a key that unlocks all meaning. But because it recognises human agency in art, it's a tenacious and useful principle. And if there is such a thing in American cinema, Scorsese is an auteur, a maestro. Along with the simultaneous transformation of the studio system with its ranks of heavily supervised long-term contract employees, auteurisme helped foster a director's cinema, offering directors, in principle, greater independence and freedom (see Contexts: Industrial & Production).

One test of the auteur was the production of an *oeuvre* – that is, a substantial body of mature work bearing his signature, both stylistically and thematically: the dynamos of original expression in a formula-bound industry. Movies were analysed for the typically recurring traces of an auteur's hand. This risked praising directors for simply repeating themselves, leaving a clear pattern for analysis in auteuriste terms, while neglecting the more versatile studio professionals, whom narrow

male group dynamics

authorship theory patronised as mere metteurs-en-scène – journeymen directors.

Scorsese has both the *oeuvre* and the range. He has editing and writing, and even acting, as well as directing skills. *GoodFellas* is certainly 'Scorsese territory', and lines up eloquently alongside his other New York/gangster pictures in its fictional exploration of a real criminal subculture. But he has made documentaries, a classic-novel adaptation, commercials, a remake of a 1950s' suspense movie, a Paul Newman vehicle, and an educative television series.

Not all were Scorsese 'projects', nor were all successful. The issues that attract Scorsese – the relation between self and environment, male group dynamics, divided identities, the conflict between the spiritual and the material, 'the insults and the worries' of everyday sociality – can be presented through a number of scenarios. They are adaptable to time and place. Nevertheless, at the solid centre of Scorsese's *oeuvre* are those movies set in contemporary or recent urban America, mostly in New York, which track in vivid episodes the lives of urban criminals.

An ironic bonus for garlanded auteurs has been that their names can become descriptive labels applied to films made by others – 'Hawksian', 'Fordian', etc. These days French film criticism has no qualms about using the term '*Scorsesien*', underlining his magisterial influence. It seems apt to borrow and anglicise the term, glossing not only *The Sopranos* but movies as different as *Donnie Brasco* (1997) and *Bobby G Can't Swim* (2000) as 'Scorsesian' (see Contexts: Intertextuality).

# cinematic background

*Mean Streets* (1973) made Scorsese's name. It was a 'personal' film, and a remarkably mature one. For all his range as a director, and the unavoidable compromises later, its style and concerns effectively constitute a signature that resurfaces throughout his career, most prominently of all in *GoodFellas* (this aspect is dealt with more extensively in Narrative & Form and Contexts).

'It's all bullshit except the pain'

## MEAN STREETS

The autobiographical input in his films has been readily acknowledged by Scorsese: 'In my neighbourhood the people in power were the tough guys on the street, and the Church. The organized crime figures would tip their hats to a priest and watch their language, and they would have their cars and pets blessed.' That memory feeds into *Mean Streets* (1973), with Charlie (Harvey Keitel), one of a group of Italian-American hustlers and minor criminals, caught opportunistically between a semi-articulate sense of grace (or damnation) and acting as a local enforcer for his Mafia uncle. Charlie is 'mobbed up', and the audience overhears Charlie's troubled dialogue with himself - 'It's all bullshit except the pain'. But it's the loose cannon, Johnny Boy (Robert De Niro), who nails him: 'Charlie likes everybody and everybody likes Charlie. Fuckin' politician.'

*Mean Streets* counts as an explosive intervention in American cinema, the unmistakable sign of a fresh talent that won over the stern doyenne of American reviewers, Pauline Kael. It has a low-budget 'rough' look, fast cutting, lots of mobile hand-held camerawork, improvisations, profane and often barely audible 'Wassamaddawichoo?' dialogue, no plot to speak of. It lacks an orthodox hero and heroine and the action dribbles away in the inconclusive aftermath of a street shooting, without closure. Nobody seems to have learned anything, and there is no feel-good factor to cheer the viewer. Nearly everything has gone wrong. As the final images darken, a honkytonk piano bangs out the chords of 'There's No Place Like Home' with tinkling irony, just as the travesty of a popular tune concludes *GoodFellas* (see Style: Music.)

*Mean Streets* is a fine film in its own right, not a rudimentary sketch for *GoodFellas*. It's a source movie all the same. The action, the setting, the riveting, naturalistic performances, the rapidly edited switches between violence and humour, and the music - the ambient 'noise' of modern civilisation - constitute a fictional 'world' with its own imaginative reality: a cardinal sign of authorship. But making the fiction 'real' for audiences as they watch means working an illusion, and the apparatus of this illusion resides in the formal elements of cinema.

# narrative & form

# film narrative

Narrative has long been a staple of Hollywood cinema. As a cinema of entertainment it has catered to the worldwide appetite for stories. It manufactures *motion* pictures, after all, and narrative is a kind of movement. Story is usually at least as vital as spectacle in the formation of the Hollywood product.

Narrative is closely associated with genre (see Contexts: Genre), and like genre it is where consumer demand meets a mode of production. The international movie market devours narrative, and Hollywood's graphic fictions, served up for consumption by a mass audience, depend on it. Anti-narrative cinema is associated with experimentalism and minority, even cliquish, audiences.

Narratives always need to be shaped and structured, to have a beginning, a middle and an end (though not, as the French director Jean-Luc Godard has remarked, necessarily in that order). Hence the central role of narrative *form* – defined by Bordwell & Thompson as 'a type of filmic organisation in which the parts relate to each other through a series of causally related events taking place in a specific time and space'. The general, though not invariable, pattern for classic Hollywood cinema resembles Todorov's basic model: the disturbance of an initial equilibrium by 'complications', followed by the resolution of the conflict and the establishment of a compensating equilibrium. Narration here is sequential, an 'unfolding tale'.

Such narratives can be viewed as formally and politically conservative (see Style: Realism), because they lay to rest the complications they have raised by restoring an imaginary harmony. 'Narrative closure' – the erasure of contradictions in the **dénouement** – solves all problems and 'recuperates' any radical or subversive implications in the plot. Order, and the *status quo*, are preserved.

the pattern of high tragedy

Any quick survey of movie plot structures will show this abstract model works for many films and genres. In the Western the town is cleaned up or the promised destination reached despite all hazards; in romantic comedy the couple, parted by misunderstandings, are reunited in the final scene. In the melodrama characters are tortured and purged by suffering, redeemed by hope or fortune.

And in the final scene the gangster dies.

## THE 'CLASSIC' GANGSTER NARRATIVE

Gangster movies make up a prodigious genre, with countless variants and offshoots. There is no single paradigm. But in the earliest gangster movies, and many since, a linear narrative structure takes the shape of a rising and plummeting graph: the Rise and Fall, or Life and Death, of a Gangster, plotted by a sequence of typical actions.

It's common for the gangster hero to start out small, entering a criminal subworld as a willing novice. Thereafter his commitment wins favour with the gang boss, his original mentor, whom he eventually supplants by cunning and ruthless ambition. His success in turn excites the ambitions of others and he is destroyed by rivals or the law, or by a combination of them, plus his own *hubris*. The pattern is akin to the pattern of high tragedy, though the gangster's achievements are inevitably tarnished by the fashion in which they have been won. He is worse than 'flawed'.

This biographical structure, chronicling the stages by which a hoodlum ascends through a criminal hierarchy and is finally overthrown, has a made-for-Hollywood narrative appeal. The gangster is disruptive by definition, a thorn in the side of the law, and no closure is more final than death. The pattern is elegantly simple. What's more, the biographical format can also incorporate social issues, including the eternal question of conditioning: does a man choose to be an outlaw, or is he pressured into it by circumstances – poverty, prejudice, ignorance, injustice, family strife?

Different answers are suggested in different films. There is no doctrinaire Hollywood 'line'. In *Public Enemy* (1931) establishing documentary shots

homage to hard-boiled crime fiction

of the Chicago stockyards picture the city as raw and bleak, and the young Tommy Powers is sent to the saloon for beer for his brutal cop father, a signifier of his early corruption by the slum environment. But in *Angels With Dirty Faces* (1938) two school friends and fellow altar boys make opposed choices. Rocky Sullivan (Cagney) and Jerry Connolly (Pat O'Brien) both grow up in a New York Irish ghetto. One becomes a gangster, the other a priest – each, after his fashion, a 'man of honour'. This is an outcome not explained by a socially determined view of the criminal career. Closure is effected when Rocky goes to his execution, feigning cowardice so as not to be a hero to his youthful admirers, while Father Connolly with equal nobility prays for his soul.

Just as the representation of the criminal varies, so no one narrative model can be a template for all narratives (one weakness of the structuralist method of analysis is that it prioritises similarities over differences). There are always variants at any given time, and narrative structures alter historically in the currents of social change and changes within the film industry itself. Hollywood's general conservatism, logically derived from its commercial imperatives, has to be balanced against the talented impulses within the industry that have always pushed for formal and aesthetic innovation (see Contexts: Industrial & Production).

## THE INFLUENCE OF FILM NOIR

Scorsese borrowed the title of *Mean Streets* from Raymond Chandler's famous essay 'The Simple Art of Murder' in deliberate homage to hard-boiled crime fiction and its cinematic counterpart, the **film noir**. There is an active critical debate over how noir should be defined, but that it is 'dark' (visually and in mood), that it hinges on criminal transgression and that it regularly reworks traditional Hollywood narrative forms and visual style are broadly agreed to be among its salient features.

Fractures of linear narrative – flashbacks, dreamlike interruptions, out-of-sequence episodes – frequently appear in film noir along with other sophisticated narrative devices such as the voice-over and subjective camerawork. Sometimes the narrative becomes so tortuous that it switchbacks through labyrinths of obscurity. Unconditionally happy endings are rare. The notion of a single, objective, dependable reality is challenged not just by the content of the film but in the telling. Betrayal, deception, sudden violence, tabooed desires, urban paranoia and all the themes film noir shares with the gangster genre are reflected in a narrative complexity that often leaves the audience, as well as the characters, in doubt. Noir is proof that Hollywood in the 1940s could make films that trusted the audience's intelligence.

In fact there are many films noirs that *are* gangster pictures (noir is not a genre of itself), borrowing the innovative devices of noir to complicate the strict biographical framework with its clear parabola of rise and decline.

From film noir as well as from later sources come the narrative and editing methods of *GoodFellas*. Rather than developing a smooth, continuous flow, they interface non-sequential scenes and counterpose clock time with personal or experiential time. **Jump cuts** (see Style: Editing) speed up and fragment the storyline. Past and present can be recombined so as to stress the vectors of irony, fate or choice.

Voice-over in film noir offers a running commentary of the action by the protagonist or one of the principal characters. Often it is a retrospective voice, bitter, confessional or nostalgic – e.g. the voice of a dying man in *Double Indemnity* (1944) and of a corpse in *Sunset Boulevard* (1948). It may be the voice of a man who has finally, too late, understood what has happened to him. In some instances it resembles a 'talking cure', like the patient's narrative on the psychiatrist's couch.

Voice-over is also a device associated with news and documentary, 'captioning' what the viewer sees. Such voices are never quite neutral, and in film noir they may be self-deluding; they still remain a testament of experience, bearing a phenomenological value, even when they contradict what is shown on the screen. They don't 'lie' to the audience. The voice-over is not an infallible guide, but it attaches the audience to the speaker through the illusion of personal testimony, and hence to his narrative track.

Film noir of the 'classic cycle' (1941–58) has secured a place in the pantheon of world cinema. It is no museum piece, though. Film noir in

'alienation and obsession'

the postmodern age continues to be a creative source of movie rhetoric for contemporary film-makers, Scorsese among them (others are David Lynch and the Coen brothers).

Alain Silver and Elizabeth Ward have argued that primary in film noir are the themes of 'alienation and obsession', the dark side of modern society (and the individual psyche). Dreamlike or dislocated narration suits film noir as much as its distinctive mise-en-scène. It acts as a formal correlative for the haunted minds of its plummeting characters. The audience 'sees' with the dislocated senses of their deranged **alter ego** on the screen – as in the latter scenes of *GoodFellas*, where rapid cutting and abrupt changes of locale mirror the madness of Henry's drug-fuelled desperation.

# goodfellas' narrative & chronology

In a number of his most memorable films Scorsese has worked close to film noir, revising its effects and adding topical concerns and fresh insights. In particular, he has been drawn to chronicle the city subcultures of young male criminals among the informal sociality of street and bar life. Here time isn't measured by the routine limits of the working day – as with the 'average schnooks'. Moreover, it's a synonym for a prison term. In Scorsese's urban-paranoia films of the 1970s, the jagged, episodic narratives of *Mean Streets* and *Taxi Driver* echo the nervous, alienated rhythms of their principal characters' lives. Much of their time is spent killing time before the next outburst of anger or violence.

*GoodFellas* builds on the narrative form and the editing of these earlier movies. It deserts purely linear narrative, the story told in strict chronological order, for a more dramatic and discontinuous storyline and adds the dual perspective of Henry's and Karen's voices-over. This partly parallels the interview format of Pileggi's book (see Contexts: Source Book/True Crime), but cinematically it has other meanings in conjunction with the image-band.

an inches-thick wad of bank notes

The narrative of *GoodFellas* segments time into 'windows', sequences that display vivid and fast-moving tableaux of gangster group dynamics, with Henry as the viewer's guide and reflecting consciousness. Time shrinks or expands in tune with the irregular movements of criminal life as the wiseguys hustle for deals.

These sequences are mainly in chronological order, but they jump time; the intervals vary. The first and shortest section, and the only one presented out of order, is captioned 'New York, 1970'. After the titles, plain white captions identify the initial time and place of each narrative section. They are:

■ 'East New York, Brooklyn, 1955'

In this sequence, the young Henry (played by Christopher Serrone) begins moving away from his family at home to full-time association with Paulie's mob. A series of formative encounters illustrates his induction into the gangster life. They end with a **freeze-frame** on Henry surrounded by smiling wiseguys after his first bust. The rite of passage has remodelled the boy's identity and given him a new 'family' of older males.

■ 'Idlewild Airport, 1963'

The opening shot is of Henry, loudly dressed in a more casual, updated version of his first mob outfit as he and Tommy prepare to steal a truck. 'Stardust', a sweet and rather melancholy Hoagie Carmichael song from 1929, is playing and the world seems to be Henry's oyster. Events accelerate now he is a proven operator (the mobster's pride is to be a 'good earner'). The main caper is the Air France robbery, but it's not a big climax. The narrative interest is in the growing complications of Henry's alternative families as he gets rich and marries Karen, whose own viewpoint is first heard in this section. The last scene gives a picture of the marriage as transaction, a 'deal' almost, Karen trading Henry a blow job for an inches-thick wad of banknotes.

■ 'Queens, New York, June 11th 1970'

Beginning in the early hours with the celebration of Billy Batts's release from jail, the signs of violent disintegration multiply. After Batts is attacked, the opening scenes are revisited, via a breakfast-time encounter with Tommy's mother (played by the director's mother) where all are comically on their best behaviour in the sacred maternal home. But Batts's death, the killing of Spider and Henry's infidelities, which finally push Karen to threaten him with a gun, expose cracks in both family structures. He's told to patch it up with Karen, but there is little positive suggestion that his ways will change.

■ 'Tampa, Florida, Two days Later'

Sent to Florida to terrorise a bookie into paying up money he owes, Henry and Jimmy are jailed, after it turns out that their victim's sister is an FBI employee. In prison, Henry continues his entrepreneurial career by dealing dope smuggled in by Karen. She is getting no help from Paulie or the mob, who live well inside, and is bitterly angry that Janice Rossi has been visiting Henry. Emotional wear and tear as well as separation has diminished the romance between Henry and Karen.

■ 'Four Years Later'

The disintegration continues and accelerates. Henry moves Karen and the children into an opulent new home, expands his drug business and starts getting high on his own supply with Sandy, a new girlfriend. The Lufthansa heist is carried off, only to sow dissent and enmity among the wiseguys. Killings – first Morrie, then others – thin the cast. They culminate in the execution of Tommy for killing Batts, a made man. It appears like an augury of further deaths.

■ 'Sunday, May 11th, 1980'

(Subdivided by nine time markers from '6:55 am' to '10:45 pm')

This section covers Henry's day as, wired and desperate, he tries to keep his operation afloat, ferry his disabled brother from hospital, supervise the cooking of the family dinner, appease Karen, ensure that Lois gets her hat and evade the law. His frantic movements are closely monitored by a police helicopter, and his efforts to control events hopelessly vain. (There's a touch of earlier crime movies like *High Sierra* (1941) and *White Heat* (1949) in the hunting-down of the gangster hero by police organisation and technology.) The sequence culminates forcefully with a

a pistol in her panties

gun at Henry's head, while Karen flushes away the blow and hides a pistol in her panties as the police prepare to burst in. By now arrest is almost a relief to Henry.

■ 'The Aftermath'

Charged with supplying drugs, Henry is freed on bail only to realise that he is on his own and in jeopardy, paid off with a pittance by Paulie and prone to be killed by a paranoid Jimmy. In the sterile, impersonal setting of an office suite, no carpet joint, Henry and Karen negotiate their deal with the FBI, intercut with the arrests of Jimmy and Paulie. Henry appears in court testifying to secure their conviction, then – in a break with the overall realist tenor of the film – addresses the camera directly, reflecting on his loss of the good life. In a fast cut, Tommy pops up to spray the audience with bullets; finally a set of end-titles tells the subsequent history of the three mobsters.

The use of establishing captions is not new. They save time and their specifics give an illusion of authenticity. They are found both in documentary, as an informative accompaniment to factual images, and in films such as caper movies, where a 'countdown' amplifies tension and suspense (in Stanley Kubrick's superb heist picture *The Killing*, time markers are spoken by an urgent, doom-laden, unseen 'voice of authority'). Both functions contribute to *GoodFellas*. They support the realist effect while simultaneously indexing the emotional tempo of the film, anchoring time to Henry's (or Karen's) state of mind.

The opening scene – which is far from an equilibrium – of *GoodFellas* is virtually a cliché of the genre, a gangland execution. But it's placed out of the conventional narrative order, beginning the film *in medias res*, so that during the noncontinuous but sequential narrative which follows the credits the audience already knows what Henry's youthful ambitions will lead to in 1970. Panic, betrayal, violence and death are in from the start. No honour or solidarity is apparent.

*GoodFellas* tracks the breakup of the gang as its own unstable dynamics and the closing-in of the soulless FBI fracture its tenuous unity and kill off or checkmate its members. Finally the single option for Henry Hill lies

'Character' ... is a problematic concept

between getting whacked out and entering the Witness Protection Programme as a monkey's paw for the FBI. The rise-and-fall matrix remains, but *GoodFellas* is less about the rise and fall of a gangster than the rise and fall of a gang, or rather about a volatile network of shifting affiliations among characters with varying, sometimes incompatible interests.

# character

'Character' in fiction as elsewhere is a problematic concept, though a popular one. 'Character' can mean personality, firmness of purpose, the typical or essential self, a 'colourful' person. But it also means almost the opposite of some of these: a made-up being, in film scripted by a writer and impersonated by an actor. (And a 'character actor' is one whose roles tend to be limited to stereotypes.) Yet in popular cinema as in literature 'character-creation' is one of the tests of talent. In this local and specialised sense fictional characters succeed with audiences because they are lifelike (or 'larger than life').

Character, in short, is an illusion. But the illusion is necessary to realist fiction and an important emotional tie between popular movies and the audiences. And while characters have to convince at the immediate level, allowing the suspension of disbelief, they tend to be emblematic of broader values as well. The energy of attraction or dislike exerted by characters is therefore part of a film's ideology (see Contexts: Ideology).

There are films (Science Fiction, notoriously) that dispense with characters as 'real people', just as there are critical methods unconcerned with characterology. Structuralist approaches such as Vladimir **Propp**'s taxonomy of 'narrative functions' or Claude **Lévi-Strauss**'s articulation of binary opposites look beyond character in the familiar humanist sense. But they don't pretend to explain the pleasure of the text, or account for audience emotions, such as empathy and identification, which are linked to the perception and enjoyment of character.

Yet character still has a **semiotic** value. It *signifies*. As representations characters are intricate clues, not necessarily to the real world, but to the agendas which govern the representation of the real.

a pathological mind-set

## GANGSTER TYPES

Stereotyping in art can never be completely avoided. Indeed a typology of traditional, well-worn figures goes along with generic cinema. Probably the best-known gangster stereotype is the megalomaniac: Tommy Powers in *Public Enemy*, Rico in *Little Caesar*, Cody Jarrett in *White Heat*, Al Capone in more than one film of the 'second gangster cycle' of the early 1960s (see Contexts: Genre).

The megalomaniac's single hunger is for power, for being Mr Big (often he is physically small). He is psychotically driven and can't believe in his own downfall. In his case the dedicated criminal career is ascribed to mental instability. The top gangster is a psycho, or becomes one. He lives and dies by the gun, the emblem of pure power. There are also usually subordinate psychos – sadistic hoodlums and the like – who supplement the picture of crime as the product of a pathological mind-set.

The rational criminal, on the other hand, operates on a more calculated risk and reward basis. Like Alonzo Emmerich in *The Asphalt Jungle* (1950) he may see a well-planned, one-off crime as the key that unlocks a dream, not as a regular way of life. He is nonviolent and may well have an established presence in the straight world. He may only be making an investment, not taking an active part, in the caper or heist. Risk itself doesn't excite him.

These are polarities and there are many shadings between them. Increasingly, as the gangster genre has developed since the 1970s, and especially in Scorsese's work, the emphasis on psychological realism has polished and refined the earlier stereotypes. Paul Cicero is the boss man in *GoodFellas*, but he has no Napoleonic delusions. He shuffles around like a small employer. Tommy's sporadic psycho mode is pinned to his masculine insecurities. Jimmy, the rogue outsider, has been too abused to trust anyone. And the framing viewpoint on the gang is Henry's. Henry never dreams of power, only of wealth and privilege – of *consumption* – and is increasingly irrational in his pursuit of them (see Contexts: Lifestyle & Consumption).

In *GoodFellas* residues of the old stereotypes have not disappeared, but they recur in a context that focuses less on psychopathology or the

# group dynamics

considered, actuarial approach to crime than on the everyday, intimate sociality and business of the gangster group.

# group dynamics

Character does not exist in isolation, it's a social identity, and one of the great strengths of Scorsese's mob movies is their fluent portraiture of group dynamics. A gangster, by definition, is a member of a group, and his character is inevitably shaped by his association with other members of the group. What's more, the pull between individual interest and collective values is prone to become particularly tense in a milieu where illegality is the norm and due process unavailable: no rules of evidence, no jury system, no court of appeal. It easily becomes a contest between survival and loyalty.

The four principal characters in *GoodFellas* – those who feature on the posters and publicity – are a band of semi-autonomous individuals, carefully differentiated in their attitudes to their criminal lives. The 'code' that bonds them, if there is one, is vague and loose. Jimmy names it as 'Never rat on your friends ... and always keep your mouth shut'. This is the mythical ideal; but the film proves that it cracks under stress.

Paulie, as the local godfather, carries authority in his physical presence without bluster or rage. Paul Sorvino's solid, jowly features project the watchful composure of the stern, wise father. On his first appearance, he quells the joshing and horseplay at the cabstand without a word; Henry's voice-over comments 'Paulie might have moved slow, but it was only because he didn't have to move for anybody'. Paulie's caution and secrecy preserve his distance from subordinates as well as maintaining his security, and his boss status is visually underlined by the image of Henry holding an umbrella for the gofer who is handling Paulie's telephone calls from a public phone booth.

The kingpin of the local outfit is represented as sober and clear-sighted, not just a bully but a skilled negotiator, ultra-cautious but not paranoid. Paulie's 'cool' quality emerges in the deadpan humour with which he affects not to understand Sonny's problem with the Bamboo Lounge and to have no power over Tommy. The scene is presented without commentary by Henry, but the audience understands – as the characters all understand – that Sonny is being squeezed and the beneficiary of the squeeze will be Paulie, who is acting out a bogus, helpless sympathy. His underlying ruthlessness is then displayed by the rapid and systematic looting of the restaurant and its torching once its assets have been brutally stripped.

With the pressurised business methods goes the social conservatism of the middle-aged Catholic gangster. 'Family' is sacred, parental roles are god-given, and Henry is bluntly ordered back home after walking out on Karen (see Contexts: Religion & the Family). He can do what he likes, explains Paulie (male adultery is viewed as a fact of nature), but he must return to the nest, where his male authority will cool off a dangerously angry wife. The verdict of senior management is not to be argued with (and in any case matches Henry's own basic attitude). Paulie's authority holds – even in jail. But he is finally vulnerable to betrayal.

Jimmy Conway is introduced as a 'flash', gregarious charmer, already a kind of subcultural legend: wayward, wired, a chronic thief and killer from his early years, buying popularity in the restaurants and night spots (almost an upscale version of his role as Johnny Boy, removing his trousers to get attention). Unlike Paulie, whose methods are at heart a shadowy mirror-image of legitimate business, his attraction to crime has a psychosexual edge: 'What he really loved to do was steal .... Jimmy was the kind of guy who rooted for the bad guys in the movies.'

Jimmy is set apart by his Irishness, his mood swings, his air of the lone operator not always in key with the group ethic and, increasingly, as his own greed and external forces expose the fault-lines in his personality, by his willingness to kill. Jimmy, as Henry observes, doesn't like sharing. The huge take from the Lufthansa heist obsesses him and he sets out to exterminate anyone who might have a claim or serve as a witness. Paulie turns his back on Henry once Henry is arrested, paying him off with $3,200. But Jimmy will have no compunction about murdering both Henry and Karen if he can. It's Jimmy, rather than Paulie, who drives Henry into the Witness Protection Program and the destruction of his surrogate fathers in court.

Jimmy almost always seems hyper or withdrawn, nervously unbalanced. He moves, with little warning, from congeniality to rage and violence, and the implication – highlighted by de Niro's fine performance – is that he is repressing a personal history of abusive trauma (made explicit in Pileggi's book) that erupts uncontrollably at times of high tension. Daring and successful as a robber, he is wired for disaster. His paranoia mounts with every triumph, causing him to feel both invincible and threatened, one of the classically recurrent states of gangster psychology in cinema.

But the closer Johnny Boy equivalent, the head-case who steps on the rules and overreacts, is Tommy. The scene at breakfast with his mother, the by-play between them, says much about Tommy. No father is evident, and Tommy, already comically short, becomes a sheepish little boy who tells his mother polite, soothing lies as he enjoys her cooking. She in turn patronises him by reciting a mildly blue joke. He's grown up, but he's not. Without overemphasis, this scene sketches a history of their relationship and points at one of Tommy's motives for constantly needing to prove his virility.

If violence and murder are for Jimmy 'just business', for Tommy they are intimately personal. Any disagreement, any counter-opinion, the least suspicion of a slight, gives him a rush of blood. This is the kind of temperament most easily wound up, meaning others are constantly tempted to wind him up.

Not that Tommy is averse to some heavy kidding himself. One of the best remembered scenes in *GoodFellas* is the 'You think I'm funny?' exchange between Tommy and Henry. The comic suspense is held by sudden uncertainty. Tommy has told a comic anecdote; now he seems offended because Henry has told him he's a funny guy, launching into a sequence of aggressive questions that might almost be modelled on a police interrogation.

Henry's response is hesitant – which way will Tommy go, is he serious? – and the audience has already seen Tommy's ferocious knife assault on a near-dead Billy Batts; this is a man who can go terminally ape. The tension breaks when Henry bluffs his way out of the sticky moment, but almost at once comes the shock of seeing Tommy in psycho mode. He curses and attacks Sonny, who has humbly presented his bill, then a bystander.

The cause of Tommy's outbursts is always his hair-trigger sensitivity to possible insults, the fear of being made to 'look small'. The clearest demonstration of his ego-fixated lack of fellow-feeling is his treatment of Spider, a young menial shot in the foot for supposedly getting a drinks order wrong, then killed by a rapid blast of gunfire for back-talk that incites the others to mock Tommy. (This episode is 'quoted' in *The Sopranos*.)

Any whisper of invidious comparisons triggers Tommy's insecurity, as when his girlfriend at the Copacabana touches his buried sexual fears by unguardedly saying that a white girl could fall for Sammy Davis, Jr. Only in the case of Billy Batts, who has taunted him unreasonably and persistently, is he supported and abetted by Jimmy. But it's Jimmy who cries for him.

Tommy's childish wish for stature and importance – for manliness – are finally summed up in the idea of being a 'made man' – i.e. a fully accredited mafioso. The simple, trusting passion he invests in this dream ensures that he goes to his death happy and unsuspecting till the last second. The Johnny Boy character model persists in the dangerous, immature clown of the group, tolerated till he takes that calamitous step too far.

Henry cannot be a made man for ethnic reasons. He is set apart not only by that, but by his appetite for hustling the big amounts of money that endlessly slip through his hands to fuel his lifestyle. Henry is a generalist in crime, working both with Paulie's gang, or factions of it, and on his own account, irresistibly pulled by a hyperactive entrepreneurial instinct. His voice-over largely governs the film's point of view, but can also work in counterpoint to the visual narrative. It is mostly a story of collapse and dispersal, from 'I always wanted to be a gangster' to 'I get to live the rest of my life like a schnook'.

In their interrelations the wiseguys are always men among men, and the relegation of their women to background, nonexecutive roles (see Contexts: Gender) gives the conduct of their affairs and their homosocial

a bunch of overdressed slobs

by-play a childish, one-sided quality, like kids boasting and waving guns in the schoolyard.

# losing

By a 'schnook' Henry means a loser. In Crowell's *Dictionary of American Slang*, it's defined as 'a dope, a sap; esp., one who is too meek to stand up for his rights, bargain, or defend himself from being made the butt of a joke, taking the blame, or being cheated', whereas a 'wiseguy' is 'a troublemaker', defiant of authority. The young Henry sees the local hoods as glamorous, enviable role-models, and the early close-ups in *GoodFellas* that metonymise their élite status (clothes, jewellery, cars) project his excitement for the audience to share. But the long shot shows a bunch of overdressed slobs fooling around in the street. Scorsese carefully maintains a distinction between Henry's perceptions and the audience's, his ambition and the objective context.

Henry's ambition isn't itself aberrant. The American Dream – that catch-all concept – is a dream of social mobility. It prescribes getting on, improving yourself, making money, giving your family the best. Creating an independent business out of their hopes, talents and interests is second nature to many Americans. In Henry's case, the gangster career is his boyhood image of opportunity, because the local mob are the only examples he sees of high living and freedom from constraints. His own home is a blue-collar trap, his father a disgruntled schnook who beats him. Henry does not see overdressed slobs in the street, he sees privileged renown, and one of his first big purchases is a sharp 'wise guy' outfit that shocks his mother.

He is aspiring, in short – one of what Colin McArthur calls the 'criminal disciples of Horatio Alger', the nineteenth-century author of inspirational rags-to-riches stories for boys. At one level, Henry is entirely conventional in his outlook, always seeking money rather than power, traditionally masculine, ultimately protective only of himself and his family, apolitical and individualist.

But his drive and energy become self-defeating. The good life, recklessly pursued, turns into a humdrum, anonymous domestic existence, working

## Money is God

set hours and out of reach of good Italian food. Henry has betrayed his associates, who would have been prepared to kill him anyway, and his reward is ignominy. Everybody loses as the contradictions work themselves out and the trapped characters make what deals they can.

Overall, narrative in *GoodFellas* repeats a traditional generic paradigm, from the genesis to the Nemesis of a gangster, though it's fully contemporary in its design and its sensibility. The gangster hero is not immolated but reduced, dethroned. The vein of tragedy is absent. Money is God. Henry's gaudy universe shrinks to a dull routine in an anonymous 'midwestern town', as his incurably naïve, flat and wondering voice recites its subjective meaning. *GoodFellas* is narrative-rich, but narrative, however central, is not the whole of film. Cinema's impact rests heavily, as well, on its **specific form**, its complex variety of aesthetic resources, and above all on its visual style.

# style

# visual

In literature, style makes itself felt in the use of language. A writer may exploit the 'rule-governed creativity' of linguistic expression to develop an individual style which the reader recognises as his or her signature. Style is typically associated with an author's individual personality and viewed as the hallmark of a distinctive talent.

Yet to be intelligible, any expression in words ('utterance') must observe the rules of a given language, or 'master code'. Readers expect coherence as well as a stylish performance. A language code is elastic enough to permit individual expression, yet it does set limits.

Cinema uses language as well as images, music and noise. Words appear as dialogue, as captions and titles, and as **diegetic** 'texts' (books, letters, advertisements and so forth). But the visual character of film is generally taken as primary – moving recorded images are the 'specific form' of film, tv and video.

Images are not like words, variable according to language system. The English word *dog* is *chien* in French and *hund* in German. But a picture of a dog will be understood by someone who speaks any or none of those languages. Images (or 'iconic signs') share no master code. And, strictly speaking, no exact equivalent exists in cinema to linguistic terms like 'vocabulary', 'grammar', 'syntax' or 'punctuation', though they may be useful analogues in describing what might be called the 'rhetoric' of cinema. Hence it has been said of cinema that it is 'a message without a code'. Instead, cinema has evolved, rather empirically, a variety of codes that do the work of the technical elements of language. For instance:

■ Lighting codes

These shape audience reactions: think of the backlit glamour goddesses of MGM in the golden age, or the threatening *chiaroscuro* of **film noir**

fat, ugly and foreign

### ■ Casting codes

These inject meaning through the presence of iconic stars, who bring along memories of other roles – and casting against type can be effective too.

### ■ Editing codes

These control the narrative tempo and suggest relationships by juxtaposition (as in a basic shot/reverse shot dialogue sequence).

### ■ Camera codes

These inflect meaning by angle, distance and movement: the shot from below stressing authority, the significant close-up, the sudden pan across a mesa where the Apaches are lining up.

### ■ Colour coding

This is often a source of expressive signifiers – as in the rich, extravagant tones of Douglas Sirk's melodramas that enhance his critique of the hollowness of affluent America in the 1950s.

These are examples, not an exhaustive list. The point is that cinema, in parallel with literature and other arts, finds the basis for style in the technical resources of its own medium, primarily the presentation of moving images. Films make coherent narratives out of these images, thanks to a repertoire of codes which are understood, at some level, by film-makers and audiences alike.

These codes are not immutable or everlasting, otherwise cinema would be in stasis. They also are culturally produced, and no more neutral than language is. They often carry inbuilt assumptions (it's no accident that many villains in mainstream movies are fat, ugly and foreign). Yet they do allow movies to be 'read'. They do provide scope for stylists (though it was also possible in **classic Hollywood** to speak of a 'studio style'). And they do supply a productive framework for the analytical study of film. I propose to deal with the role of style – visual and otherwise – in *GoodFellas* under five cardinal headings: Mise-en-scène, Iconography, Editing, Dialogue and Music.

# mise-en-scène

Bordwell and Thompson define mise-en-scène as 'All the elements placed in front of the camera to be photographed: the settings and props, lighting, costumes and make-up, and figure behaviour'. It is what the audience sees on the screen, the ensemble of visual elements within the frame which the editing process strings into a sequential narrative. Mise-en-scène is vital to an analysis of style, since it crystallises on film what were originally only the typed words of a screenplay.

Because a script can be filmed in a variety of ways, mise-en-scène entails choices, and choice is inevitably a key factor in cinematic as it is in literary style. Camera position, lighting, where to place the actors, set-dressing – these are all ultimately the director's responsibility; and all require a sense of style. Style is a determinant of meaning, and the technical options taken by a director help fix the significance of the mise-en-scène and shape an audience's understanding of what it sees.

Scorsese is on record as saying that 'GoodFellas is going back to the same period as Mean Streets, the early sixties, to the world I grew up in.' It is not Manhattan, and criminal ambitions have risen, but the milieu is comparable. Many scenes and stylistic touches remind the audience of Mean Streets, conveying the feel of a semi-closed society existing within a 'normal' city neighbourhood. Scorsese's point of departure is **semidocumentary** observation; but not clinical observation. His style leans to the sensuous and emotional; his viewpoint is more involving than contemplative.

This general involvement, though, is compatible with moments of relative distance, assisted by the voice-over and **freeze-frame** techniques. After young Henry torches the cars of a rival cab company, he runs from the explosion towards the camera as Johnny Boy did after cherry-bombing the mailbox. And because the voice-over does not explain precisely what is happening (Pileggi's book spells it out), the attack seems, like Johnny Boy's, to be wanton and impulsive. The freeze-frame isolating Henry against an expanding fireball pictures the boy raising forces more powerful than himself. The explosion appears to be blowing him into a future of violent criminality.

# mise-en-scène

## a song of teen romance

As the freeze shot holds, Henry is heard talking of the 'respect' he has won – the gangster's euphemism for fear and intimidation. In the next shot he appears outfitted in his brand-new gangster threads. As the camera sweeps him from head to toe, it adopts the viewpoint of his shocked mother. Clothes like this mean dubious sources of income. At this point crime rewards Henry, while estranging him further from his natural family.

The freeze-frames are intended to register moments of insight or awareness, sudden epiphanies, stepping-stones on Henry's journey from teenage gofer to mature, seasoned hood. They graphically underscore the impact events and personalities have on him: his father strapping him for truancy ('everyone takes a beating sometime' is his later reflection), the mobsters proving they have greater muscle by rough-housing the postman, Jimmy Conway introducing himself to Henry with a big tip and a frank gaze.

These shots are not elegantly framed or lit; they suggest the album snapshots that record personal lives, captured instants from the past, subjective memories. The last view of the teenage Henry, though, is an objective group portrait that includes him. After his first bust, he's surrounded by Paulie and the gang, one of them, no longer the apprentice, an accepted goodfella.

In the three-minute sequence shot that follows Henry and Karen from their car to the dinner-and-show evening at the Copacabana, the Steadicam threads its way behind Henry and Karen through a crowded, busy basement. The shot takes in the behind-the-scenes bustle and Henry's first-name familiarity with the ranks of service and kitchen personnel, before it settles them, exhilarated, at their front table. They consume, effortlessly, while the workers wait on them. Flunkeys above stairs and kitchen hands below picture the disproportions of a bloated leisure economy, lubricated by lavish tips.

Throughout the scene the Crystals' hit 'Then He Kissed Me' is heard playing. The soaring wall-of-sound orchestration half-drowns the dialogue. It's a song of teen romance, which both highlights and undercuts Karen's enchanted awe at this gaudy world of privilege. No wonder she asks Henry 'What do you do?'

Then the camera swings left from the seated couple to take in Henny Youngman (played by his much older self) cranking out the routine sexist jokes of the old-time, stand-up comic – 'I take my wife everywhere but she finds her way home' – and his cheesy patter continues over a cut to Idlewild. Karen hears the (non–diegetic) song, but not the prophetic latent warning of marital neglect in Youngman's act.

Three minutes makes an exceptionally long shot, though Scorsese isn't wedded to the long take; elsewhere in *GoodFellas* a hectic narrative pace is maintained by rapid cutting. Throughout the movie, fluent, mobile camerawork makes visible the concealed workings and infrastructure of Henry's world, not only its active criminal schemes.

Mise-en-scène in *GoodFellas* is thoughtful rather than showy. It is never allowed to overwhelm narrative. As in *Mean Streets* and *Taxi Driver* the frame is often crowded with incidental detail or marginal action. Scorsese's interest in the wiseguy subculture at large, not in its leading lights alone, makes him alert to the visual texturing achievable through a semidocumentary technique. It's an approach that suits moments of intimacy or secrecy, 'exposing' the inner world of an enclosed group just as a popular subtype of true crime (see Contexts: Source Book/True Crime) exploits the inside stories of informers and ex-criminals. The peering, prowling camera observes the wiseguys in their environmental bubble, the air they breathe. It picks up the faces that come and go, the ceaseless hustling and deal-making, the male camaraderie.

Equally, it can disclose subdued emotional currents and social tensions. At a dreadful 'hostess party' to receive Karen after her marriage, the camera retreats from the older woman and young children at a dining table to reveal Karen, the fish out of water, among the mobsters' wives. Wearing a delicate yellow dress, she sits among the other women's atrocious hairstyles and 'thrown together and cheap' outfits – 'pants suits and double knits' – in muddy or garish greens, blues and reds. The probing camera details the coarseness and vulgarity of the gathering, in

# mise-en-scène style

key with Karen's voice-over commentary. Rapid close-ups of her face and eyes register the strain she has to suppress.

This is not an artless, point-and-shoot technique. Scorsese has made documentaries and knows the difference between documentary and feature film. It's a practised employment of contemporary cinematic realism, a realism no longer bound to steady compositions, classic establishing shots and a single viewpoint for the audience. Yet *GoodFellas* is unquestionably a generic movie (see Contexts: Genre), emerging from a generic history as well as a real-world subculture. And the genre exerts its own influences on the style, just as the style reworks the genre.

A good clue to Scorsese's aesthetic principles emerges from his comments on *The Last Temptation Of Christ* in *Scorsese on Scorsese*. Contrasting his version of Christ's passion with George Stevens's *The Greatest Story Ever Told* (1965), he remarks:

> Stevens' film had an antiseptic quality about it, a hermetically sealed holiness ... Jesus talks about forgiving everyone, but ... He's just someone who glows in the dark. He doesn't understand my suffering. Stevens did have the brilliant idea of using the American south-west, with the Grand Canyon standing in for Israel [sic], but here is Jesus speaking to thousands and they all manage to hear Him! What we did ... was to stage these scenes with small groups so that He was heard by all. In Stevens' film there's a self-conscious emphasis on design ... no sense of real people living. I think the pictorial aspect – the pageantry – took over.

The grand, sculptural, Hollywood-epic style is not Scorsese's. The immediate, sensuous feel and look of his most accomplished films becomes a conduit for repressed fears and conflicts, instants of change or realisation, a climate of strong but transient feelings. This applies whether or not religion is attached to the plot, in the despiritualised landscape of *GoodFellas* as in *Mean Streets* (see Contexts: Religion & the Family). Both movies focus on what gangsters do all day, and the scrappy in-between moments are given more attention than the major heists. Yet Scorsese's New York wiseguys are recognisably Hollywood gangsters, remixing and updating the classic recipes of a popular genre (see Contexts: Genre).

# iconography

Very often Scorsese's mise-en-scène is 'busy', crowded, a canvas packed with detail, colour and movement. Images can be painterly, but they are not dwelt on. The pictorial value of each shot, however brief, is maximised. The **iconography**, rather than the more abstract, formal properties of composition, tends to predominate.

Iconography in this context refers to the recurrent visual signifiers that earmark a genre. The Western features horses, saloons, typical landscapes and six-shooters, while the gangster movie's iconographic checklist includes, in Colin MacArthur's words, 'dark streets, dingy rooming-houses and office blocks, bars, night clubs, penthouse apartments ... firearms, automobiles and telephones'. MacArthur adds:

> The automobile is a major icon in the gangster film/thriller. It has a twofold function in the gangster film: it is the means by which the hero carries out his 'work' ... and it becomes, like his clothes, the visible token of his success.

In *GoodFellas* the locales are not the stately haunts of the Corleone family. They represent a much more localised, loosely structured and informal kind of criminal business that extends from selling cartons of cigarettes at factory gates to multi-million-dollar heists. The local cabstand and pizza parlour furnish Paulie's headquarters; domestic environments are solidly well-off lower-middle-class Italian-American, a cultural space replicated even inside jail; the streets are average 'neighbourhood' city streets, not dark and mysterious labyrinths.

The high life for Henry and his associates doesn't mean gate-guarded mansions but the carpet joints, glamorously furnished, heavy on attentive service and classy entertainment, and commonly fronts for

obvious phallic connotations

illegal gambling. When he wants to impress Karen (and show her off) he takes her not to a funky restaurant but to the Copacabana, where priority treatment is guaranteed.

Gangsters have guns, and use them. They are tools of the trade, with obvious phallic **connotations**. Tommy above all is fast on the trigger, the munchkin with worries about his masculinity. But guns in *GoodFellas* are not always respected icons. Towards the end Henry totes a collection of them around for sale in a paper sack only for a contemptuous Jimmy to turn them down as unsuitable. (Again, *Mean Streets* is invoked: Michael failing to offload the Japanese converters he'd bought in the ignorant belief that they were German lenses.)

More problematic is Karen's relationship with firearms. She admits that when she first handled one 'it turned me on' – not just sexually, it's implied, but by a sense of power. Later, she is on the verge of shooting Henry for his infidelity. Finally – and its seems almost like a joke on the phallic woman image as the true-crime magazine covers display it – she stuffs a pistol into her knickers to conceal it from the invading FBI.

The luxury tastes of the wiseguys seem to mirror the consumerist concerns of the 1980s and 1990s, as if the wiseguys were proto-yuppies, though the showy apparel is traditional for movie mobsters. Men in the macho mould, they strut like peacocks. Stella Bruzzi has noted that

> here are characters who have both cultivated an aggressive image and are immensely vain, and whose sartorial flamboyance, far from intimating femininity or effeminacy, is the most important sign of their masculine social and material success.

For Bruzzi, the film's central nexus of violence and wealth is 'a fusion epitomised in the loud glamour of the mob's clothes'.

The men's fashions themselves constitute a code, flaunting criminal affluence in a style opposed to the understated subfusc dress of the law-abiding banker or accountant. They are also, like the food the wiseguys eat, Italian-derived. *GoodFellas* is rich, too, in images of succulent meals: oiled sausage on a barbecue, fresh ice-packed lobsters delivered to prisoners, a sauce that must be cooked exactly right. And though the mobsters deal in food for profit, it also remains a pleasure to be enjoyed for itself. It induces a relaxed sociality, prompts a recognition of their ethnic heritage and perhaps stands as the one genuine aesthetic experience in lives that have little time for culture in the extended sense (see Contexts: Lifestyle & Consumerism).

Cars in *GoodFellas* are still both functional and status symbols (though the Internet Movie Database lists some anachronisms among the models), but the telephone has become more of a menace than a convenience. Once a vital instrument of gangster logistics, it has now been turned against the mob, thanks to heavy (and often illegal) wiretapping. Paulie won't have one, and (as in *The Sopranos*) the public phone booth becomes a signifier of the gangster's justified paranoia.

The contradictions of the gangster's world are deep and deadly. His icons are also his potential downfall. Jimmy, who flashes money around, is angrily horrified at the uncool sudden acquisition of cars and mink coats by other mob members. The gangster likes to put on a show, to draw attention, but his big-spending habits may betray him. The telephone may be the conduit for an enemy spy. And, in the end, whoever lives by the gun must be prepared to face dying by the gun.

Location shooting in *GoodFellas* supplements the semidocumentary feel. This is not quite Warshow's 'city of the imagination', abstractly represented by nocturnal skyscraper blocks. It lacks the tense, romantic excitement generated by the expressionistic landscapes of film noir. Where the wiseguys live is a no-account neighbourhood, anonymous apart from its ethnic flavour. Its prevailing cultural tone is summed up in Morrie's amateurish toupee commercials.

Yet the proximity of a tenuous and vulnerable space, Idlewild Airport, means that a fantastic store of plunder lies on the doorstep. The movie's two big capers are the Air France and Lufthansa robberies. This twist of the genre's iconography reinterprets the modern city through its original representation of the airport. It's no longer a modern communications centre or leisure escape route, but a local Aladdin's Cave for serial exploitation. The location of the airport, too – out of the city centre, bordering on the nondescript – almost defies any sense of community.

# editing

Thelma Schoonmaker first worked with Scorsese on *Woodstock*, edited *Who's That Knocking At My Door?* and after a hiatus due to her lack of a union ticket has been his editor on every feature since *Raging Bull*. Their joint editing skills mean that *GoodFellas* is both pacy and dramatically well proportioned. **Jump-cuts** slice through time and space and captions save a lot of laborious exposition. The voices-over colour the meaning of scenes with their retrospective commentary. Compared with, say, *The Color Of Money*, fairly conventional and one-paced, it flashes along with increasing impetus.

The clearest exploitation of this method is seen in the 'May 11th, 1980' section, when ultra-mobile camerawork and fast, jagged **montage** become the formal correlatives for Henry's drugged and disordered state of mind, speedy in all senses. Sixteen feverish hours are covered in eight minutes of screen time as his reality becomes an indiscriminate jumble of urgent tasks and nerve-jangling frustration. In his fragmented condition, though hustling drugs, he never dreams that the men in the helicopter chasing him are 'Narcs'.

*GoodFellas* moves fast, though not at a uniform pace, including long takes and tracking shots as well as rapid montage and narrative jumps. An assured sense of structure and purpose – of how the parts contribute to the whole – allows the story to progress along a firm narrative line, while much of the action is loose or incidental, almost like the riffs of jazz improvisation. Robert Kolker chooses a musical analogue to describe the editing techniques of *GoodFellas*:

> Scorsese's editing style is carefully executed and tuned to create the appropriate dramatic rhythm of a given sequence. The angularity of the cutting, making arhythmic joins between the movement in one shot to the movement in another, speeding things up ... provide a kind of rhythm section for the shots that together compose the movement and meaning of the film.

The final proof of the editing quality lies in the general recognition that though *GoodFellas* runs at about 140 minutes, when seen, it doesn't seem like a long film. Everything seems to take the right length of time. At a stage in American cinema when many feature films prolong themselves well beyond the point of serious narrative interest, this is a tribute to *GoodFellas'* style as well as its absorbing content and the continuing vitality of the crime-based movie.

# dialogue

The tough-guy idiom and street slang of the urban criminal gang was developed in the pulp magazines of the 1920s, a vital source of creative popular writing. It is a heightened and concentrated version of the conversation of big-city alpha males, fast and punchy and wholly American, though enriched by immigrant lexicons and speech-patterns. It can be a language of pointed threat and insinuation as well as violent abuse. The pulp writers seized on the expressive impact of spoken American. Dashiell Hammett rendered it raw and terse, Raymond Chandler poeticised it. It continues to flourish in crime fiction: in the more polished contemporary thrillers descended from the pulps, and in the crime-film genre.

*GoodFellas'* dialogue, like the eternal challenging banter in *Mean Streets*, is largely a discourse of competitive virile egos – 'ball-breaking'. At times it's pathetically artless and juvenile ('Yeah, yeah, yeah! Come on! Come on! Come on!' yells Billy Batts), and it has a limited emotional range. The wiseguys mumble and repeat themselves, break off, change tack in mid-sentence. Their vocabulary is alternately colourful and hackneyed, and among them the rhetorical question ('Guess what?'; 'Do you believe this?'; 'What can you do?') is a popular tic. It's uneducated street speech, the speech of men who value words below action.

Far from being a crude, restricted code, though, it commands a battery of adroit and complex linguistic ploys. When Tommy decides to bluff Henry with a show of straight-faced heavy kidding he is far from laconic. Like Paulie in his subsequent godfather-scene with Sonny, Tommy builds up his macho act with the cadenced repetitions and rewordings of Italian-American speech.

# dialogue

sentences rattle out like bullets

It's a dextrous performance that involves juggling words, playing on differential meanings of the word 'funny', Socratic questioning and a disarming denial of hostility while the sentences rattle out like bullets, inhibiting a reply. There's a purpose in the tease: to test Henry's manhood. At first Henry is abashed, and the viewer feels the electric uncertainty. Then he breaks the spell not through a rival display but with the kind of throwaway insult that will later get Spider killed – 'Get the fuck outa here, Tommy.' He won't take Tommy seriously; but what if he had? Would he have been glassed like Sonny or shot like Spider?

The long-delayed liberation of language from a genteel censorship in the late 1960s was a boon for screenwriters. The naturalism of the dialogue in *GoodFellas* would be diluted if the wiseguys couldn't say 'fuck.' When the ears of adult filmgoers were protected from words that could be regularly heard in school playgrounds, movie gangsters may have talked tough but they were never openly obscene.

Now they are, and audiences are no longer infantilised by Bowdlerisms. But the emphatic punctuation of habitual swearing isn't necessarily monotonous. In *GoodFellas* it contributes to the mood-music while presenting the everyday foul-mouthed chatter of the male group as a feature of their masculine identity. In public at least, profanity isn't shared with the women, and when Billy Batts, the honoured old-timer, swears in front of Tommy's girl Lisa, he adds an automatic 'Excuse my language.'

A lot depends on inflection as well as content, as illustrated in another mob picture of the 1990s, softer-centred but highly Scorsesian and also 'based on a true story.' *Donnie Brasco* devotes one scene to an undercover cop's explanation of how an old hit-man's catch-phrase 'Forget about it' can be said five different ways, with variant meanings. Similarly, in *GoodFellas* words can signify differently, or evoke alternative responses, according to their tone and context.

But language has its limits. Gangsters are not lawyers who fight forever with words. They are men of action. Sooner or later the words exhaust themselves, giving way to homicidal violence.

# music

The first announcement of a new presence in American cinema for viewers of *Mean Streets* in 1973 was to hear 'Be My Baby' blasting out of the screen virtually before the film had begun. The rich Motown sound, the sexual come-on, the funky urban feel to the song and the unusual conjunction of sound and image bands appeared as the signature of a film-maker who recognised the vitality of popular music. Music has always been part of the texture of Scorsese's movies.

The first song heard in *GoodFellas* is the corniest of ballads, 'Rags To Riches', performed by Tony Bennett, the lounge tenor who had established himself in the late 1940s, with full orchestra backing:

> I know I'd go from rags to riches
> If you will only say you care,
> And though my pocket may be empty ·
> I'd be a millionaire.

Bennett, himself the son of an Italian father and a golden testament to the national dream of talent and hard work as guarantors of success, caresses every word.

But the irony is inescapable. Wealth is the American metaphor (or substitute) for love. As in *The Great Gatsby*, cash and emotion, nominally opposed, are exchangeable forms of one another, like the twin faces in mob territory of intimidation and 'respect'. The dripping, sentimental song fits Henry's impressionable consciousness, and his awed infatuation with money and privilege, at the same time offering a distance on it.

*GoodFellas'* other musical bookend is 'My Way', Sid Vicious trashing the glib, sententious lyrics of the pub-belter's standard, lounge music's equivalent of Kipling's 'If'. It's a song that Frank Sinatra, another Italian-descended singer of the pre-rock generation, had made almost a personal anthem. It celebrates a self-serving myth of the full, accomplished life led by the heroic individualist, battling through adversity unswayed by mass opinion, as the 'final curtain' approaches. Vicious brilliantly pounds it to extinction.

a sardonic judgement on his self-deception

It's the right musical finale to *GoodFellas*, a telling ironic counterpoint to Henry's early dreams of criminal glory. The old mob style is passing away in the age of Reagan and globalised crime. Henry, far from being an indomitable free spirit, has painted himself into a corner. He's done it the robbers' way and is now doing it the cops' way. Freedom is out of sight.

Scorsese has said that he 'wanted to take advantage of the emotional impact of the music', not simply use it 'to establish a time and a place', though equally 'the only rule was to use music which could only have been heard at that time' – i.e. no anachronisms.

As usual his choice is **eclectic**, ranging from Alfredo Di Stefano to Italian doo-wop, soul and rhythm and blues, replacing the themed orchestral score with an anthology of popular tunes and arias. Scorsese has noted that plenty of old favourites stayed around on jukeboxes until well into the rock era, and these tend to be the tunes heard earlier in *GoodFellas*, while Henry's nightmare Sunday in 1980 plays to the sound of drug-influenced rock. Henry's release from jail is a cue for another Tony Bennett number, 'The Boulevard Of Broken Dreams', a classic elegy for wasted expectations; soon 'Gimme Shelter' accompanies the cutting of the cocaine. When FBI agents raid the Hills' house, the television is showing Al Jolson's 'Toot Toot Tootsie, Goodbye' from *The Jazz Singer* (1927), the first talking picture. Later Karen will dump the cocaine.

The supple and varied use of music helps define the emotional register of the film, thicken the atmospherics of a subworld and measure the historical distance from the 1950s to the 1980s. Popular music in all its rock-derived forms has gone from rags to riches since the mid-1950s, commercially and artistically. The show tune and the products of Tin Pan Alley are passé, or for some nostalgic. At the same time pop and rock have become a cynical and exploitative industry. By the time Henry rats on the mob, a hobnailed punk assault on 'My Way' sounds like a final statement of vacancy as well as a sardonic judgement on his self-deception.

The tie-in album is now a must for any film with ambition, a prime marketing and promotional tool. The result is many albums of tunes that, severed from the movie which held them together through their relation to a visual narrative, give the impression of an oddball, random collector's hand at work. Conversely, the thoughtful weaving of songs into a movie can illuminate and extend meaning, exploiting all the possibilities of cinematic style.

# realism

Scorsese has gone on record with his aims in *GoodFellas*:

> I knew it would make a fascinating film if we could just keep the same sense of a way of life that Nick had in the book ... to be as close to the truth as possible in a fiction film, without whitewashing the characters or creating a phoney sympathy for them .... Throughout the picture I was telling people, 'There's no sense in making another gangster picture, unless it is as close as possible to a certain kind of reality, to the spirit of a documentary'.

Realism is a slippery issue for a number of reasons. For one thing, cinema is both a recording medium and an expressive form. It 'captures' reality by the optical-chemical process, giving the camera the status of an objective surrogate for the human eye. It also – intentionally or not – inflects reality, freighting what it records with a particular meaning and value. It selects even where it doesn't invent. In this it is like still photography, which puts reality in a shaping context. Snapshot albums and home movies embalm real memories. They also help support a family ideology. Formal studio portraits, though true-to-life, emphasise dignity and order.

**Semidocumentary** is one kind of realism, if realism is considered as a play of formal devices. Scorsese adopts the home movie, cinema in its humblest form, to establish the characters at the opening of *Mean Streets*. There they are, performing amiably for the camera, just as real people do. It makes them 'real'. But it's a trick, a filmic illusion making a fiction credible.

a vision of breakdown and futility

This illusion is the great strength of realism, though it has often come under critical attack. The status of realism not just as mimesis – 'lifelikeness' – but as an ideological function of art has been queried by film theorists who find it politically unsatisfying. In this view, realism (to paraphrase a complex argument) beguiles the audience with a view of reality as free of contradictions and therefore unchallengeable, presenting as true and permanent what is actually the product of particular social-historical forces. In Roland Barthes' words, it 'naturalises history'.

Too often this critique undervalued the independent-mindedness of an audience (see Contexts: Audiences). But alongside it ran a fresh interest in the formal apparatus of cinematic realism. In **classic Hollywood** this included features like 'invisible editing', eye-level camerawork, linear narrative, location shooting where possible, a single, stable viewing position for the audience. The conventional feature film offered, in the end, a reassuring commonsense world just as the 'anti-traditional' style of film noir served a vision of breakdown and futility.

But if realism is never value-free, it should follow that it can be employed critically rather than only to support the illusion of a single, self-sealing reality. This is certainly how practitioners have seen it, seldom as a transparent, one-to-one equivalent for reality. Scorsese, for example, insists on the verisimilitude of his technique in *GoodFellas*, yet he has also called it 'an indictment'. It's an unavoidable self-contradiction for any artist. Representing reality also means having an angle on reality, interpreting it, taking sides. Realism in art is the formal execution of an aesthetic ideology, not a perfect mirror.

Equally, realism itself is an historical product. Like any other modality in art it is subject to change as conditions change. The semidocumentary look, switchback narration and rapid editing of *GoodFellas* would not have been recognisably 'realistic' to a golden-age audience.

Besides that, no film need settle for a uniformly realist mode. Near the end Henry turns in the courtroom to address the camera, breaking the 'fourth wall' rule, while in the final image Tommy reappears to spray the audience with gunfire, in a sudden, unestablished shot. In fact this rule is not a rule but an expedient convention, and has been broken a thousand times. Contemporary postmodern culture has made texts that ignore realist logic or mirror their own fictional field of reference almost commonplace (see Contexts: Intertextuality).

Certainly there are aspects of *GoodFellas* that are **meta–cinematic**, alluding to other films or to the working processes of movie-making. However, Scorsese is not postmodernist in the prevailing sense of deserting realism for fabulation and intricate formal play; rather, these aspects indicate how the terms of realism can shift in a society saturated with signs, texts and images.

# contexts

# context's role

It's a requirement of critical understanding to place a film in its context – or, more, accurately, contexts. Contexts extend as a field of relevance well beyond the specifics of a given film and the immediate contributions of the individuals concerned. More than a penumbra of associations around a film or a loose gathering of topical references, they amount to the sum total of conditions under which a movie is made. Also, the passage of time alters and expands context, especially in relation to the viewer's experience of the text. If you can't step into the same river twice, audiences can't view the same film twice. Context is potentially infinite, but always exceeds the personal aims and efforts of a single auteur. Film is **polysemic**, and a movie's meanings aggregate from multiple sources.

Infrastructurally, film is business. **New Hollywood** may not be **classic Hollywood**, but the industrial basis of movie-making remains. Films are capital-intensive and geared for profit, even if many fail. They are marketed to audiences as commodities to be consumed for pleasure. But works of art (or 'cultural products') are unique commodities. They have no material use-value. They exist in the realm of thought, feeling, imagination, sense-impressions and meaning. In short, a movie is an ideological experience.

# ideology

Bordwell and Thompson explain ideology as 'a relatively coherent system of values, beliefs and ideas shared by the same social group and often taken for granted as natural or inherently true'. Ideologies (capitalism, Communism, religious denominations, etc.) favour definite interests, but may conceal their partiality to appear universally acceptable and unchallengeable. In film, ideology appears in the form of representations

GOODFELLAS

of reality, a fictional parallel world that invites the viewer to share its map of reality.

In one sense, the ideology of Hollywood film is simple. It's capitalism, the religion of the market entailing class and labour divisions, where the bottom line rules. But films are highly mediated products, never straightforward reflections of a dominant system's values; a dominant ideology implies alternative ideologies, also seeking expression. It is challenged by them as well as its own internal contradictions. Only the crudest propaganda delivers a single message. Ideology is less a message than a way of seeing the world, necessarily biased and possibly mystifying, but communicated and 'lived' as if true.

# social representations

## GENDER

Among the clearest examples of the ideological 'spin' that films can exert are the changing representations of ethnicity and gender. In classic Hollywood, a black star would have been unthinkable; African-Americans were deemed 'naturally' subordinate to whites. Blacks appeared in minor roles, as faithful servants, comic buffoons and the like. At best, they were sympathetically represented for their loyalty to a white superior (sometimes they still are). Now vital struggles have been won and black actors like Denzil Washington and Will Smith play major roles.

But they are black *male* stars. The situation of women, another outgroup, is not fully comparable. Always necessary to Hollywood as audience magnets, women stars were simultaneously flaunted, objectified, as spectacle, and condemned to find their inescapable destiny in standing by their man. Stringent polarities of the good woman and the *femme fatale* projected (often with vivid power) not women as they were, or could be, but women as they appeared via the partial and restrictive suppositions of patriarchy.

Thirty years after the stirrings of second-wave feminism, the passive, domestic woman is not the regular feminine ideal in cinema as, under pressure, an ideological shift has generated new female character types.

she'll always be vulnerable

This has not usually brought thoughtful feminist heroines to the screen, but it has favoured 'feistiness', greater selfhood and an enlarged sense of independence. In the ideological conflict between these qualities and other needs, women have struggled free of the older stereotypes into the dilemma of the 'divided woman'.

This was a major theme of the **néo-noir** *Klute* (1971) and lay at the heart of Scorsese's *Alice Doesn't Live Here Any More*, Ellen Burstyn's project and her successful Oscar bid. It resurfaces in *GoodFellas* in the representation of Karen as a mob wife. Like everything else, her relationship with Henry degenerates as the romance wears off. Karen, a strong personality, isn't long-suffering about this. She can nag and accuse, even mix it up with Henry in exchanges of domestic violence. What she can't do is leave him. She abides by the wife-mother role. She risks smuggling drugs into prison for him. She finally accepts that, as a Jewish daughter, she can never see her parents again. Thanks to Henry, she'll always be vulnerable, even if they separate.

But she has bought into his world, and now experiences the payback. It's Karen's voice-over that records the effect of an ideology in naturalising a particular world view: the criminal lifestyle becomes 'normal'.

True to life? Probably; ideology doesn't have to falsify. What liberated woman would wish to keep company with a gang of unreconstructed male supremacists? It would stretch the film's premises to represent Karen otherwise, and her own voice tells the audience that she finds the life exciting. But ideology lives in what is excluded as well as what is represented. *GoodFellas* is critical by implication of Karen's treatment; what it never suggests is that there might be serious alternatives to her cat-and-dog married existence with Henry. (In *The Sopranos* a more tortuous, Freudian relationship is explored, between the professional woman and the slobbish Mafioso.)

In the end, the men run the show; if not admirable, they are prominent and powerful. This is the way of their world. One of Scorsese's words for *Mean Streets* was 'ethnographic'; he has called. *GoodFellas* 'anthropological'. While not literally true, they are terms relevant to the study of a subculture, a male group bonded by a shared identity, values and lifestyle. A lot has been written about the buddyism and homosocial bonding rituals common in American cinema, its gay undercurrents and its privileging of male friendship over heterosexual romance. But there are few Hollywood movies – some war and prison pictures, for example – that exclude women. They are, so to speak, unavoidable nuisances. Groups seeking or guarding definition generally rely on another to define themselves against.

In *GoodFellas* women are not wiseguys. They collude with their menfolk's criminal activities and benefit, or suffer, from them; they don't plan heists or run rackets. Their importance, in the cast and in the narrative, is second-rank. They aren't encouraged, or allowed, to take initiatives.

The gangster's mother reappears, less pious but still the provider of a spiritual comfort zone and home-cooked food. Molls are now the casual or kept girlfriends of the wiseguys whom they take out on ritzy Friday nights, adornments of the gangsters' parade and the living proof of their success. They are expected to watch their mouths. Lois, Henry's 'mule', is a bothersome flake who won't go on a cocaine run without her special hat. Karen, who had attracted Henry because she stood up to him, flushes away his stash in self-protection and is physically punished for it.

The wiseguys are shown as unreconstructed alpha males, Americans with Mediterranean machismo in their blood, inheritors of an earlier tradition of patriarchy (the older ones still throw Sicilian phrases into their conversation). Among them a family ideology is strong, but it's sealed off from their appetites. Above all, they call the shots. Their will is paramount, not to be debated. When Henry rolls home drunk in the early hours and gets an earful from his mother-in-law, he doesn't argue. He gets back in the car.

These men are not morally superior to their women, but they are far more empowered and they lead exciting, active, self-indulgent lives. The wives' lot is to keep house, raise children and fill the rest of the time somehow. The girlfriends are arm-candy and bedmates. Penned into a close circle of acquaintance, limited by archaic definitions, the mobsters'

proud of their Sicilian ancestry

attachments in *GoodFellas* are manifestly not role models for the twenty-first-century woman.

## ETHNICITY

If there's no honour among thieves, there are supposed to be rules and principles. When Jimmy Conway tells Henry what the two most important things in life are, he's conveying to the boy that outside the law personal trust is imperative – you can't sue for breach of contract – and reinforcing the code of *omertà*. *Omertà* is the manly code of silence, derived from the Italian for 'man'. The principal characters in *GoodFellas* are heavily Italian-American and proud of their Sicilian ancestry. Henry and Tommy, 'outsiders' who liaise with the Mafiosi and pay tribute to Paulie from the proceeds of their own crimes, share Irish blood.

From the birth of the genre gangsters were heavily coded as non-**WASP**. The visual medium created an expectation that the gangster should appear as aberrant as his trade, and the use of strong-featured actors remote from the contemporary male ideal helped fix the physical prototype of the gangster. Cagney's looks, and his character in *Public Enemy*, are Irish, while Edward G. Robinson and Paul Muni were both Jewish, but their names in *Little Caesar* and *Scarface* are clearly Italian. (Bogart, a WASP and more ethnically neutral in appearance, found it easier to graduate to saviour-hero roles in wartime.)

There were admittedly real-world antecedents for this exercise in stereotyping. Prejudice and discrimination against the later waves of immigrants – mainly from southern and eastern Europe – flourished among older-stock Americans. Official and ground-level resistance to immigration could block opportunities, as it had done for the ambitious Jewish immigrants and second-generation Americans who had found the new cinema industry easier to enter than established businesses. Despite the melting-pot cliché, assimilation was not always welcome on either side. Excluded non-WASPs were driven to form communities, subcultures and businesses of their own – in some instances, criminal subcultures that could become, at least locally, a kind of secret government.

chronically and unthinkingly racist

Al Capone, the most famous of gang bosses, was Neapolitan rather than Sicilian, but his image overshadows the popular conception of the Italian-American top hood, florid and jowly. His relations with other ethnic gangsters were decided by gang politics: he struck up a bootlegging partnership with the Jewish Purple Gang in Detroit and resolved his consequent dispute with the Chicago Irish mob under Bugs Moran by the St Valentine's Day Massacre. Twenty years later, the US senator, Estes Kefauver, rather than referring to the Mob or the Mafia, recorded his wish to 'put the Frank Costellos, the Joe Adonises ... the Zwillmans, the Anastasias, the Marcellos, the Guziks and Accardos, the Tony Gizzos, the Mickey Cohens, the smug Jimmy Carrolls and Kleinmans and Rothkopfs – and all the rest – out of business.' The sonorous roll-call of Irish, Jewish and Italian names carries a covert charge of UnAmericanism, a popular slur during the Cold War.

Rivalry and warfare among ethnic gangs were common – in Roger Corman's retro-gangster film The *St Valentine's Day Massacre* (1969) they hurl insults like 'greaseball' and 'mick' at each other – but their shared **otherness** on film encodes ideological fears. The suspicion of foreignness still clings to 'hyphenated Americans'. Despite Hollywood's commercial sensitivity about representing Italian hoods in movies (the word 'Mafia' is notoriously avoided in *The Godfather*), this otherness is finally inseparable from the ethnic screen gangster's identity.

What Scorsese does in *GoodFellas* is to register the fading of ethnically based values over a generation as criminal enterprises expand and diversify and America itself swerves towards a more divisive and gangsterish ideology of economic relations. The relentless pursuit of money, a substance free from ethnicity or even nationality, supplants the warm and orderly environment of inherited customs.

The wiseguys themselves, like the petty hoods of *Mean Streets*, are chronically and unthinkingly racist. Charlie dodges a date with a beautiful go-go dancer because 'she's black'; Tommy slaps down his girlfriend for a remark that offends his white skin; Henry's foolhardy belief in his own immunity takes the form of a commonplace racist

He dies for his mistake

dismissal of black men: he asserts that only black robbers go to jail as a result of their ineptness.

This is *hubris*, which Henry pays for when he's arrested for rough-housing the bookie in Florida. But it's later given an uneasy, two-way application by the fact that Stacks Edwards, the single black character hired for the Lufthansa robbery, does exactly what Henry says blacks do: he falls down on the job. Edwards's no-brain incompetence is retained from the screenwriters' stripping down of Pileggi's book (see Source Book/True Crime). He dies for his mistake, half-awake and dopy in a tip of an apartment.

No fellowship there; but neither is it at a premium among the wiseguys. The film's overall perspective is cynical about the codes of honour and silence they profess. Though they collaborate to rob and terrorise, there is no spiritual solvent, no active ideological consensus to unite them when it counts, not even heartfelt religious belief. There's only the baseline capitalist credo of individual interest.

## RELIGION & THE FAMILY

The religious ideology of screen gangsters has usually been Catholicism, and Scorsese's Catholic background is often cited as a key to his work, especially its interest in guilt and absolution. The initial voices-over in *Mean Streets*, shared by Harvey Keitel as Charlie and the director himself, reflect on these issues, albeit in existential rather than strictly religious terms: 'You don't make up for your sins in church. You do it in the streets.' And there are intermittent reminders of a Catholic immigrant culture through the cut-in sequences of the festival procession. Charlie may not be a good Catholic, but he can't sever himself completely from the theology he was raised on.

In *GoodFellas* religion recedes to the faintest of ambient murmurs. No one debates the relative weight of the spiritual and the material. It's a foregone conclusion. Only the material is real. Henry hides his birth religion from Karen's parents and he has no problems with a Jewish wedding. Priests are invisible. Meaning and purpose reside in big scores and fancy living.

Any residue of a religious attitude tends to lie in the lip-service paid to the family ideal. The goodfellas aren't bohemians or rebels. Along with their regular goals and aspirations and their *Playboy*-style leisure lives runs a belief in both the nuclear and the enlarged family as well as the criminal one. Conventional gender roles are assumed, the husband the breadwinner and the wife the housewife/nurturer. But there is no pattern of regular citizenship, no settled routine of existence, to support this arrangement, and in practice the men, married or not, behave like bachelors outside the home and regard male sexual infidelity as an automatic right.

It's a macho world, in which men 'protect' their women and children while reserving final authority to their own egos. In that way it replicates the history of the Mafia itself and its quasi-feudal role in offering the use of its power to the weak – at a cost. Paulie and his kind may police the wiseguys; men police the marriage.

Mark Winokur has noted the ambivalent quality of the ethnic criminal family in gangster films of the 1980s and 1990s: 'On the one hand these films seem to validate the closeness and eccentricity of the ethnic family ... But the family also emerges as an institution that encourages family psychosis.' Crime as a way of life magnifies the stresses of a family system already prone to fracture and breakdown in late twentieth-century America.

In principle, marriage doesn't suit the gangster archetype any more than it does the Western hero. In early gangster pictures women are generally either molls or mothers who only marginally feminise the environment. In many, the protagonists trail an aura of sexual deviance or inadequacy. The trigger-happy gangster can serve as a case study of the little man with the big gun who fears female sexuality. But in *GoodFellas*, with the exception of the dwarfish and mother-eclipsed Tommy, the gang are average macho males who reject nurturing roles and please themselves with women as they do with their other entertainments, while – as a montage of still photos demonstrates – clinging to 'family values'.

off-the-shelf diamond geezers

# culture

Crime and gangster pictures continue to ride a wave of popularity, and have become internationalised. British audiences have been able to sample the home-grown, though Hollywood-influenced, variety in a succession of hard-nosed thrillers since *Get Carter* (1971). The mobster heroes are generally cockney hard men, continuing the association of crime with the big bad city, as in *The Long Good Friday* (1980) and *The Krays* (1990); more recently they appear as the off-the-shelf diamond geezers and cartoonish East End thugs of *Lock, Stock And Two Smoking Barrels* (1999) and *Snatch* (2000).

Global organised crime is kept in the headlines, in part a substitute for Cold War paranoia as a source of external threat and agitation. Political meltdown in the former Soviet bloc has seen the KGB spies, once cherished by western film-makers, metamorphose into Russian Mafiosi. Prohibition has returned as a focus of gangster activity thanks to the giant profits available from the illegal drug trade still not remotely containable by a wasteful and counterproductive 'war on drugs'. The standard plot line for a crime film these days is drug based. Drug trafficking, along with its corollary .money laundering, is the global bootleg commerce. It is a thriving link between mobs of all descriptions and a gift to the world movie market.

Even so, America holds the patent. Historically, the Italian-American gangster, importing the corruption of the Old World into the New or bending the American dream to his low purposes, has had the highest and most authentic profile. For this, Hollywood has to take much of the credit. Al Capone used to complain that 'there's a lot of grief attached to the limelight', but he warmed to the idea of his magnified screen image in *Scarface*.

Gangsters weren't new in Hollywood pictures in 1930. They had appeared with some frequency during the silent days – as early as D. W. Griffith's *The Musketeers Of Pig Alley* (1912) – and the formalist director Josef Von Sternberg had boasted, with typical exaggeration, of making the first gangster film in *Underworld* (1927). But the true generic matrix for the

ambitious, ruthless, and doomed to die

organised crime picture had to wait till Warners initiated their gangster
cycle in the early 1930s. From then on, what John McCarty calls 'the
movies' love affair with the mob' made gangsters and their cinematic
*alter egos* intimate companions.

# genre

The gangster film in its most recognisable form was initially a product of
Warner Bros in the final years of Prohibition and the early ones of the
Great Depression. Warners was an inventive studio, commercially and
creatively, though not a big-spending one like MGM. Under its dynamic
head of production, Daryl F. Zanuck, it not only inaugurated the gangster
genre but developed the stars who would play the necessary
'sympathetic heavies' – Humphrey Bogart, James Cagney, Edward G.
Robinson.

Warner Bros' promotional slogan was 'stories from today's headlines' –
raw, topical and immediate subjects giving a realistic feel to fast, action-
driven narratives of organised crime. Edgar G. Robinson in *Little Caesar*
(1930) and James Cagney in *Public Enemy* (1931) established the
prototype of the gangster hero – ambitious, ruthless, and doomed to die,
not just as a moral lesson to the audience, but by the logic of his own
career path. Though in neither case was ethnicity made a foreground
issue, Rico Bandello and Tommy Powers were unmistakably of Italian and
Irish descent. In 1932, Howard Hawks's *Scarface* (not a Warner
production) featured Paul Muni as Tony Camonte in a role manifestly
based on Al Capone; subtitled 'Shame of a Nation', it underlined the
psychotic element in the gangster chief, with latent but definite
suggestions of incest. Paul Muni's theatrical, high-energy performance
stressed paranoid derangement and coarse, animalistic drives.

In this trio of movies, as Colin McArthur writes, 'the genre reached a
point of classical development unusually soon after its appearance'. In
each case the film charts the career path of an American of recent – and
Catholic – immigrant stock, whose rapid advancement due to quick wits,
thirst for power and lack of moral compunction leads to megalomania,
isolation and death.

competitive jungle

This pattern of catastrophe led Robert Warshow to christen the movie gangster a 'tragic hero', an **existential** figure struggling to dominate the urban environment which conditions him, furnishes his opportunities and finally threatens him. The gangster hierarchy is always unstable, a competitive jungle in which violence ultimately rules, and the loyalty to which outward respect is paid is never guaranteed.

The genre continued, mainly with lesser films, throughout the 1930s, in the face of pious disapproval from religious and civic groups which found the gangster hero pernicious and from a sternly watchful censorship. Other subtypes of crime film developed alongside it. One of these, as if in compensation, featured a cop or G-man as hero, infiltrating and defeating the gang in the name of democracy; the titles are symptomatic – *G-Men, Bullets Or Ballots, Racket Busters.* In wartime, the mob movie was far less prominent than pictures featuring detectives, secret agents or war itself, the ultimate male action genre. But it never quite disappeared, even if its re-emergence was postponed till *The Godfather* (1972).

There are gangs and gangs. It's possible to distinguish the ethnic mob movie proper not only from the broader spectrum of crime films, but from variants in which the criminal 'outfit' has no Mafia connections. The WASP outlaw couples in *High Sierra* (1941), *Gun Crazy* (1950) and *Bonnie And Clyde* (1967) may constitute, or work with, a gang, but they are not mobbed-up. Neither was the Midwestern bandit John Dillinger, whose story has been filmed three times (once for television). Poetically, he was gunned down by the FBI as he left a cinema.

The caper movie, in which a squad of seasoned and specialised criminals is assembled for a single job, also belongs to a type distinct from the mob film. It's a crime variant which has produced some excellent films, including *The Asphalt Jungle, The Killing* and *Reservoir Dogs.* These films, though they can be violent, rest largely on the tension and suspense that belong to the thriller. The thieves are career professionals, even if everything goes wrong with their operation, but not Cosa Nostra; they have no 'family' connection.

'affirmation of myth as myth'

The old ethnic hoods of the Prohibition era surfaced again in the 1950s and 1960s in a cycle of period reconstructions, most of which chose the biographical format. *Al Capone* (1959), *The Rise And Fall Of Legs Diamond* (1959), *Portrait Of A Mobster* (1961), about the New York gangster Dutch Schultz, all preceded *The St Valentine's Day Massacre.* These were not big productions, and they petered out, but they were engaging narratives that blended nostalgia with the traditional elements of violence, corruption, conspiracy and the rise and fall of the lead character.

The success of *The Godfather* (1972) revived the Mafia film, with examples spread over the three following decades and paralleling an interest in other classic genres or subgenres, including **néo-noir** and the 'dirty' Western. New Hollywood was refashioning Old Hollywood. John G. Cawelti, observing the trend, has suggested that there are four basic ways of reinterpreting the generic movie: 'humorous burlesque, evocation of nostalgia, demythologization of generic myth, and the affirmation of myth as myth'.

It's certainly true that genre boundaries, always fuzzy, have become more fluid than ever in contemporary cinema. The proliferation of mob movies in the 1980s and 1990s saw a range of treatments. Mafia comedies were one offshoot in the 1980s – *Prizzi's Honor* (1985), featuring the novelty of a hit-woman, and *Married To The Mob* (1988) among them. In his ultra-violent, heavily stylised remake of *Scarface* (1983) Brian De Palma turned Tony Camonte into Tony Montana (Al Pacino), a Cuban deportee torn apart by fulminating ambition, incestuous desire and cocaine madness. The film was no nostalgia trip but a postmodern update, replete with 'quotes', while *Donnie Brasco*, made after *GoodFellas* and showing its influence, clung to the mystique of honour.

Though the concept of genre relates primarily to relations between texts, rather than between them and social reality, genre is never immune from social change. The expansion of the drug market – shunned by old-timers like Paulie but a massive earner – has been met by the criminal justice system with a draconian sentencing policy and the pressuring of accused traffickers to turn informer. Since 1970 the RICO (Racketeer-Influenced and Corrupt Organisations) Act, with its crushing financial penalties, has been available for deployment against organised crime. The Federal Witness Protection Program offers a last-chance haven for mobsters who have seen their luck run out. The new legal rules have modified the generic codes.

A key strength of the gangster genre is more than ever its inclusiveness. It stands where professional crime, the legal system, business, politics and the family intersect. Because its narrative conflicts hinge on this convergence of key social structures, gangster movies, made for entertainment, always promise as well a critical perspective on American society.

## INTERTEXTUALITY

Generic films are **intertextual** by definition, even if generic definition is not an exact science. We can measure likenesses between movies inductively by considering **iconography**, narrative structures, correspondences of time and place, character typology, shared situations and so forth. But how can this be done without some *a priori* notion of what we are looking for? Increasingly problematic, too, is to set firm limits to a genre. The inter-generic, or multi-generic, film is common nowadays.

What we can say is that identifying the intertextual exchange of meaning between films, including **meta–cinematic** references adds a constructive dimension of knowledge. *GoodFellas*' field of signification extends not only to *The Godfather*, the most obvious contrast, but to a whole generic history. Place *GoodFellas* alongside, say, *Little Caesar* or *The St Valentine's Day Massacre*, and the overlaps and differences will add layers of meaning to each one.

Echoes of other movies are no longer just accidental, the product of a ready-made template. Intertextual links are explicitly made by Scorsese in shots that refer back to moments from earlier crime films. One is the Steadicam introduction of the wiseguys, as the camera weaves past them while an off-screen voice recites their names: a 'lift' from *Little Caesar*. Another occurs in the sudden shot of the 'dead' Tommy at the end, 'quoting' *The Great Train Robbery* (1903). A scene at the Sherwood Diner replicates the spatial distortions of a famous shot from Hitchcock's *Vertigo* (1958), while Lesley Stern has discovered much wider ripples of intertextual reference in this and other Scorsese films.

## LIFESTYLE & CONSUMERISM

From the vantage point of 1990, *GoodFellas* reviews previous decades, concluding in 1980, a few months before Ronald Reagan was elected President. With privileged hindsight, it seems to foresee the hedonism and acquisitiveness of the 'greed is good' era. The gangsters are appetite-driven. They want luxury and privilege: expensive clothes, fancy night spots, fast cars, designer drugs, the sense of their own public aura. This is not a revolutionary wish-list. It's the menu of consumer capitalism.

But think of what it excludes, notably the enjoyment of art and nature; the education which is forgone in favour of street-smarts; any spiritual life beyond an inherited, outward and nominal Catholicism; any serious politics and history; a broad, informed view of the world. These gangsters are not sophisticates. Their desires are suburban, and their pleasures the pleasures of tired businessmen.

The wiseguys are big spenders, and Stella Bruzzi, borrowing a vocabulary from Thorstein Veblen's *Theory Of The Leisure Class*, has diagnosed their economy as 'conspicuous consumption'. They love to display their wealth, and their appetites are astonishing. Henry consumes his way to debt and desperation, minor mob members made flush by the Lufthansa heist lash out on sudden luxuries that will betray them, lobster and champagne are shipped in to the goodfellas in jail. Even at the end Henry drools over the spoils of crime: 'We had it all, just for the asking .... I had paper bags filled with jewellery stashed in the kitchen. I had a sugar bowl full of coke next the bed .... Anything I wanted was a phone call away.'

Cocaine in the sugar bowl, jewels in paper bags – it's an incongruous picture. Its surreality underscores the fever of material desire, inextinguishable even by a cornucopia of loot. All the time an unstoppable need to generate income drives the wiseguys to push up the risk factor. And, after the end game has been played out, Henry's punishment is not death or imprisonment but, symbolically, 'egg noodles and ketchup' instead of the rich, authentic Italian cuisine he is used to.

## SOURCE BOOK/TRUE CRIME

*GoodFellas* emerges from the literary subgenre of 'true crime', 'true' meaning nonfictional. Works in this category range from serious biographical or social studies to the opportunistic and sensational. Some are courtroom dramas, some concentrate on police or forensic successes. Those at the cheaper end of the range purvey a mix of violent, grisly and salacious detail, pop psychology and a pose of moralistic concern – a formula followed by many crime movies.

Even sophisticated readers are not immune to the thrill of true crime, and publishers have eagerly fed the taste for 'inside stories', giving the transgressor a voice, allowing the reader to share trade secrets. A market for insiders' accounts of the secretive Mafia world announced itself in the early 1970s, when Peter Maas's *The Valachi Papers* (1972), based on prison conversations and billed as 'the first account of the inside of the Mafia', became a hot bestseller. A wave of similar biographical·and confessional books followed.

Pileggi's *Wiseguy* (the movie title was changed to avoid confusion with similar-sounding titles, and pluralised) is in this tradition: a piece of documentary journalism based largely on trial transcripts and interviews. The Introduction explains that the author had 'gotten bored with the egomaniacal ravings of illiterate hoods masquerading as benevolent Godfathers'. It doesn't describe the editing and selection process that reduced the copious material to book length, but it presents Henry Hill as in some ways an exceptional witness to his lawless past. Pileggi found him more coherent than the average mobster, a thoughtful man 'with an odd detachment, and ... an outsider's eye for detail'. (Though in an interview the author has said that Henry was not so much interesting as available and willing to talk.) At the same time he is cautious not to romanticise Hill:

> Henry Hill was a hood. A hustler. He had schemed and plotted and broken heads. He knew how to bribe and he knew how to con. He was a full-time working racketeer, an articulate hoodlum

> from organized crime .... It seemed to me that a book about his
> life might provide an insiders' look at a world usually heard about
> either from the outsider or from the *capo di tutti capi*, top.

Heroic, Henry is not; symptomatic, he is. Both insider and outsider (partly
because only half-Sicilian), Henry appeals to Pileggi as a medium-grade
pro criminal with good connections, no boss-man yet superior to the
illiterate plodding hood trapped in the self-serving folklore of his
occupation. Henry, it's implied, has acquired an objectivity, prompted no
doubt by his admission to the Witness Protection Program, that gives his
story unusual value.

His is not the only voice heard, though. Karen and Linda both contribute
testimony, and there are bridging sections by Pileggi summarising the
counter-moves made by the criminal justice system. The flat, functional
reporting style frames the more animated dialogue sections. It's a movie-
script half-made.

The book's Epilogue, unlike the film, makes no mention of Henry re-
offending. On the last page he's living well again, as a paid, immunised
government witness, 'the ultimate wiseguy', exempt from paying his back
taxes. But Pileggi's verdict is that 'his survival depended upon his
capacity for betrayal'. Henry couldn't get away with being a crook; he can
get away with being a rat. The shift of emphasis in Scorsese's ending
lends it a more critical and downbeat edge.

## REAL & GENERIC GANGSTERS

Just as the Western is an important subtype of historical romance, so the
gangster film is a product of twentieth-century realism in the arts.
Warner Brothers in 1930 was a studio ready to grow, but its specialty was
cheap movies with an immediate contemporary appeal.

The 'stories from today's headlines' slogan associated the new genre with
urban journalism and news events. Gangster films didn't need MGM-
style opulence, just snappy, idiomatic writing, cheap sets and actors who
could project tough-guy images as plausible and compelling as the real-
life ethnic hoods whose exploits and photos filled the papers.

## the Mafia ... 'a nationwide syndicate'

Al Capone was the celebrated crime lord of the Prohibition era, and Chicago the city most associated with organised crime. But Capone had been sentenced to jail on income-tax evasion charges over a year before Prohibition ended. The future story of the mob, as the opportunities gained under Prohibition were consolidated after repeal, would be told in terms of families and syndicates rather than single fiefdoms. Organised crime continued to expand in the period up to the Second World War along with gang wars, as rival outfits fought for the lucrative spoils. During this era there was some liaison between the American military and the Sicilian Mafia; the imprisoned mobster Lucky Luciano was allegedly enlisted by US Naval Intelligence to help prepare the invasion of Sicily.

Increased popular awareness of the Mafia – or Cosa Nostra, 'Our Thing', as the American mob preferred – grew out of the Kefauver investigations of 1951. Estes Kefauver, a senator from Tennessee, chaired a Senate Committee on organised crime in American cities. The committee had the power of subpoena, and its hearings, nationally televised, drew a huge, fascinated audience to watch characters like Frank Costello and Albert Anastasia squirm, fidget and plead the Fifth Amendment (against self-incrimination). Kefauver, a grandstanding politician who campaigned in his home state wearing a coonskin cap, drew the conclusion that the Mafia was 'a nationwide syndicate ... a loosely organised but cohesive coalition of autonomous crime "locals" which work together for mutual profit' with no 'absolute boss'.

The publicity generated by the Committee's work fed into movies like Fritz Lang's *The Big Heat* (1953), in which a smooth, cordial gang-boss runs a town, 'owning' the law and ruling through corrupt placemen as well as thugs. His name is Lagana and he has a giant picture of Mama on his den wall, but there are no explicit Italian references in the film. Italian-Americans were rightly alert to hostile stereotyping, and pressure on Hollywood by such bodies as the Italian-American Anti-Defamation League worked to keep shock-words like 'Mafia' out of pictures.

Even so, and even if Kefauver overstated the continuity between the Sicilian Mafia and its New World variant, Italian names and organised crime were regularly associated in the public mind. The famous 1957 raid on the Cosa Nostra 'summit meeting' at Joseph Barbara's house in Apalachin, New York, turned up fifty-eight men of Italian extraction, allegedly visiting their host because he was in poor health. According to Robert Lacey, '50 had arrest records, 35 had convictions and 23 had served prison sentences'.

Twenty were convicted of conspiracy, though the verdict was reversed on appeal. The police had acted on suspicion, not on legally valid evidence. The odour of suspicion that helps create the gangster's ambivalence has never gone away, and Italian-American hoods have acquired a twin identity, off-screen patriotic businessmen and on-screen Mafia. Now – as in *The Sopranos* – fictional Italian-Americans, both mobsters and citizens, discuss the effect of their representations in other fictions, such as those by Scorsese and Coppola, two Italian-American luminaries of the New Hollywood.

# industrial & production

In *The New Hollywood* Jim Hillier traces the complex of processes that transformed American film production. Factors such as the legally enforced dismantling of the old **vertically integrated** studio system, falling cinema attendances and television's home-viewing opportunities reshaped the industry in the quarter-century after the Second World War. Independent producers and agents became more active and influential players, assembling 'packages' (a script, a star and a director, for instance) for which they would then seek finance. These volatile new conditions, Hillier explains, were two-edged:

> The main advantage that independent producers had was the ability to make films more cheaply than the major studios independent producers ... [but they] had two main problems: getting finance and getting their finished film into the theatres. The two were intimately connected (as they still are): a guarantee of distribution, and thus of access to theatres, made it easier to get finance .... And this is where the new-style major 'studios' came in.

# industrial & production contexts

So the names of the old Hollywood majors appear on Scorsese's films – Warner Bros. (*Mean Streets, Alice Doesn't Live here Any More*), Columbia (*Taxi Driver*), United Artists (*New York, New York, The Last Waltz, Raging Bull*), Twentieth Century Fox (*The King Of Comedy*), Universal (*The Last Temptation Of Christ*). Underneath the labels, the product has altered. If new hybrid cinema embodied in Scorsese's most expressive films has not shed all vestiges of classic American cinema, it marks the shift towards a fresh conception of popular film. One of the most welcome aspects of the New Hollywood as it emerged in the early 1970s was the partial demolition of the cultural Berlin wall that had separated the independent or art-house film from the mass-market feature.

The film-school movie brats were instrumental in making this happen. As a film student and novice director Scorsese had learnt his craft from **classic Hollywood** as well as the French New Wave of the 1960s. He'd absorbed the work of American directors as different as Orson Welles, John Ford and Sam Fuller besides that of Godard and Truffaut. John Cassavetes, the New York film-maker who funded his **semidocumentary** independent films by acting in mainstream movies, had been a mentor.

The conjunction of structural and economic change, fresh American film-making talent, European influences, audience tastes that had been reshaped by the cultural revolutions of the 1960s and backers who were willing to fund originality sparked a kind of renaissance.

Scorsese made his first big impact with the low-budget *Mean Streets*, a success that instantly made him marketable. This is where the ambitious new director's problems tend to begin, since access to his work for the global audience is likely to depend on studio finance (Coppola's attempt at running his own studio, Zoetrope, crashed). Some collisions of interest are inevitable; even negotiated compromise can leave bitter, eternal resentments. But the dogmatic demarcation of the valuable artwork from the mass-market product isn't a helpful way of understanding contemporary American film. Since 1973 Scorsese has worked on studio as well as personal projects, and on some that fit both labels.

*GoodFellas* is one of the last group – an entertaining generic movie, distinguished by the passionate and intelligent mastery of cinematic art associated with Scorsese's best films. It was a self-chosen project: Scorsese had read Pileggi's book during the shooting of *The Color Of Money* in Chicago. Having called the author, he was enthusiastically guaranteed the film rights by Pileggi. (As it happened, these had already been snapped up by Irwin Winkler.) The two of them co-scripted *GoodFellas*, sectioning the narrative and then – in Scorsese's words – arranging the sections 'like building blocks' into a screenplay. Filming, backed by Warners to the tune of $25 million and with Irwin Winkler as producer, started after the release of *New York Stories*, in October 1989.

Scorsese's own enthusiasm and commitment show up in the tempo and energy of *GoodFellas*, when *The Colour Of Money*, essentially Paul Newman's brainchild, had looked relatively flat and monotonous. But he still had to conclude a deal with Warners, who imposed conditions. One was that the cast should include a major star, another that the finished movie would be subjected to test-screening for a **preview** audience. (It was eventually 'trimmed' for an 'R' certificate.) Hence Robert De Niro reappears in a Scorsese film after a seven-year gap, playing what is technically a supporting role, a fact which dissatisfied a number of reviewers – and perhaps some fans.

Yet *GoodFellas* doesn't play like a film in which the artist's soul has to struggle against the clichéd and philistine standards of studio bean-counters. Warners, the corporate residue of the great studio that had launched the gangster picture, were probably taking few risks with their money. Scorsese wasn't being pushed into directing a movie that had little personal appeal for him, just to keep working and earning. Often, as the mainstream co-opts innovation, so breakthrough initiatives refresh the mainstream. *GoodFellas* pleased the critics and the public. As a medium-budget movie it cost $25 million and yielded a domestic profit of around $50 million, slightly less than *The Color Of Money* and two-thirds of what *Cape Fear* would make for Universal the following year, but a gratifying amount.

By comparison, the 1990 box office rankings were led by Fox's *Home Alone*, and the top ten included undemanding star-name features like *The Hunt For Red October*, *Kindergarten Cop* and *Dick Tracy*. Two traditional genre films were listed at numbers three and four: Kevin Costner's wearying and pretentious Western, *Dances With Wolves*, and a sparky romantic comedy, *Pretty Woman*.

Hollywood, new and old, has always been in the business of second-guessing popular taste at the same time as its products seek to mould and direct it. In the twenty-first century after a hundred years of cinema, it's recognised that there is not a single audience but differential audiences, ranging from the big 'family' audience through to niche consumerships and transient cults. This state of affairs may create its own problems; but it works in favour of some diversity. Ultimately Hollywood films follow the law of the market. The paying punter decides success, however many millions are splashed out on hype and promotion. And the relations between the customer and the commodity, the viewer and the text, are complex and not always predictable.

# audiences

The box office, however wobbly and arguable the published figures, measures the financial success or failure of a film and offers clues to what pleases or turns off audiences. It does not directly explain why filmgoers like this movie and reject that one. Generic pleasures are deeply established in Hollywood film, but not every genre movie turns a profit. Stars with huge fanbases make movies that flop. What's more, the meanings that audiences take from what they watch are not unanimous. No audience is fully homogeneous.

Filmgoers are individuals, but no individual is only that. The preferences and aversions of cinema audiences – 'cultural consumers' – are bound to be determined in part by their social identity: by factors such as age, class, ethnicity and gender rather than by unconstrained personal choice. This is the very basis of 'audience targeting' – while in pursuit of a maximal audience Hollywood's native opportunism can spread the appeal. *GoodFellas* updates the male action genre by representing Linda as a 'strong woman' who is neither a tart nor an asexual old mother (classic roles for women in the gangster picture). By 1990 the prevailing assumption is that the female lead should show some spirit. Thanks to

The meaning ... of a movie is never absolute

feminism, a broadened awareness of women's reality has made the adoring, submissive model a virtually discontinued line. (The representation of Teresa in *Mean Streets* as a sad, helpless victim had drawn accusations of misogyny.)

In both films the central focus is on the men and their interactions. But not even men comprise a single audience. What is probably true is that men and women will find alternative ways of responding to *GoodFellas*. Indeed the film itself draws attention to the alternative routines of male and female sociality. Men socialise intimately with men outside the home, in bars and clubs. By contrast, the hostess party is suffocatingly domestic, and the women's talk more family-oriented. How do audiences view this in terms of their own experience and beliefs about gender?

The meaning, or tendency, of a movie is never absolute. Any film can be read in a number of ways and on a number of levels. The director may be an auteur, but his work always escapes the limit of his intended meanings, because audiences, though not free from preconceptions, are never the obedient servants of an authorial dictatorship. The simplified concept of the passive viewer on whom the film has a guaranteed one-way effect, like hypnosis, has been abandoned by modern **reception** theory. Meaning, like value, emerges from an active engagement of the viewer with the film and depends on his or her perspective as well as what objectively appears on the screen.

And *GoodFellas*, like the professionally crafted picture it is, has something for everyone in its blend of the old and the new, its eruptive violence, its rendering of a half-world with its own internal rules and conflicts, its generally sharp social observation and its adroitly paced story. It is fully artistic without threatening anyone for whom the word 'art' is a disincentive.

# critical responses

Despite six nominations, GoodFellas received only one Academy Award – for Pesci's performance – but Scorsese won the Silver Lion for best director at the Venice Film Festival, where the film premièred. Opening receipts in the US were buoyant, and the critics were near-unanimous in

the greatest living American director

their liking of the film. Most understood that it was a picture about a group and its lifestyle, not an individual hero. As the Introduction to *Scorsese On Scorsese* has it, *GoodFellas* is 'less a portrait of one individual's dealings with the mob than a vibrant, bustling canvas exploring a whole society at play with guns, money, food, drugs and unwritten codes of conduct'.

Apart from this broad consensus, some saw it as a critique of the get-and-spend ideology of the Reagan–Bush years, using the generic framework to expose a free market of the most primitive, rapacious kind. It benefited from appearing at a time when gangster pictures were in vogue, but it was formally interesting for a mainstream movie. Scorsese and Pileggi had evolved a sharp script. Its array of acting talent was formidable.

All in all, it cemented Scorsese's reputation as the greatest living American director. Though that reputation has wobbled since, most expanded critical appraisals of *GoodFellas* since 1990 rank it as an achieved and important movie. It has become a film which any serious critic writing on 1990s American cinema feels bound to address.

For Les Keyser it's both a parable of self-destruction and a spectacle of voluptuous greed. Discussing the fast-cut scenes of physical action around the shooting of Spider and Karen's spat with Henry over Janice, he writes:

> The juxtaposition also reveals the uneasy mixture of *Mean Streets* and Armani commercial that *GoodFellas* relies on. *GoodFellas* celebrates the materialistic, celebrity track, brand-name lifestyle of the Cicero clan as it dispassionately records their compulsive violence, relentless paranoia and inexorable deterioration.
>
> Duality and irony reign in *GoodFellas*. The wiseguys are wised up by the most dramatic reversal of fortune.

Keyser also registers the friction between what Pileggi writes of as the empty 'myth' of Mob honour, existing more in films than in actuality, and the use *GoodFellas* makes of the old generic code of silence and loyalty to ironise Henry's betrayal. The screen mobster's death-or-glory attitude has been supplanted by expedient survival.

Robert Kolker finds irony, too, though more in the reflexive, **meta-cinematic** side of *GoodFellas* – its play with generic reference and in camerawork and editing that calls attention to itself rather than smoothly unfolding the story (though he also describes the film as 'almost documentary'). In discussing the two levels on which he sees it operating, Kolker stresses the humour in *GoodFellas*, and concludes by comparing it to *Tristram Shandy*:

> Scorsese has created the perfect latter-day cock-and-bull picaresque narrative about gangsters, which like Sterne's novel and later modernist works of fiction and film, continually gloss their own status as fictions. At the same time, he created the perfect gloss on the gangster genre. The interaction of voices, narrative spaces, gazes at the camera, winks, nods and smiles acts to interrogate our response to the history of gangster films. Why do we believe in anything we see in gangster films? Scorsese seems to ask. They are playing out sixty-year-old narrative codes that trigger our assent to the fantasy of a powerful life.

Kolker may be right in his assumptions about audience response, but the best generic films do more than gloss the genre; they reinvent it for their age. Scorsese has admitted that he finds 'subverting' the genre difficult; his aim has been more to anchor it to his own concerns as a film-maker. Luckily, he has a sharp contemporary awareness as well as a film sense, which registers on critics like Marilyn Yaquinto. She finds in *GoodFellas* problematic issues of assimilation and identity as the old, disciplined Italian ways die: '[These wiseguys] don't live the ethnic holism of the Corleones, with their sturdy links to Sicilian traditions. Instead these hoods reflect the breakdown of the family order and the infiltration of yuppie nihilism.'

Like Kolker, Lesley Stern foregrounds the nonrealist elements in the film, such as Tommy's posthumous machine-gunning of the audience, which

'a world willed into being by obsessive desire'

support a current theoretical preference for viewing cinema as a more or less conscious reflection on its own forms and processes:

> The film is about a world willed into being by obsessive desire, it's about the reality of fantasy, about carving out a place by cutting up space. So too it is about the dangers of cinema. We witness, and perhaps are implicated in, the enactment of an obsession. All obsessions involve a theatricalisation of desire, an impulse to create a world .... The cinema, too, involves the creation of 'other' worlds, the carving up of space, a *mise en scène* of desire .... Cinematic desire, in Scorsese, can't be easily extricated from the desire to be a gangster.

Meta-cinema is all around us, in the various forms of postmodern fabulism, pastiche and filmic in-jokes, sometimes taken to the point of weary affectation, that are now a pronounced tendency. *GoodFellas* itself has been referenced in a slew of other films, including *Shallow Grave* (1994) and *Mickey Blue Eyes* (1999) as well as The *Sopranos* television series. Self-reflexive cinema that unpacks its own box of tricks is enjoying a vogue.

Scorsese can compete with anyone in paying homage to cinema in his films, but the tradition from which *GoodFellas* emerges is one of social concern as well as genre. Representations of the real in fiction are never complete, and a **semidocumentary** style never guarantees adequate knowledge of it. Yet no fiction can be understood without considering how it relates to the first-order reality which it transmutes – even if 'maps' of reality differ and the relationship is inevitably complex. All fiction is historical and points outward as well as inward.

Social concern usually entails social criticism, and gangster pictures have been free with this. Scorsese is no crusading Zola, picturing the condition of society through researching and publicising its deepest inequalities. All the same, *GoodFellas* offers a perspective on America at a moment when its foundation myths, immortalised in the lyricism of the Western, have become windy excuses for violence, plunder, treachery and unprincipled self-interest as the market ruthlessly sorts out winners and losers. On that level, it's not unreasonable to read Scorsese's energetic tableau of a small, vicious world as an epitome of the state of the nation.

# conclusion

Like many young film students, Scorsese was an admirer of Orson Welles, especially of Welles's landmark film *Citizen Kane*. Like Welles, who had to wait for a Lifetime Achievement Award, he remains an Oscar-free director. But Scorsese is a more substantial figure than Welles, whose inflamed ego resisted the tough but enabling discipline of the studio system. His urgent and profound commitment to film culture shows up in his campaign to preserve nitrate stock, and in his *Personal Journey* television series. He's been called a commercial director: no shame at all in that title, if it's taken to mean that he's a gifted and serious artist who wants his work to reach a big, popular audience rather than a clique of acolytes. Unlike Welles, he has a modern conception of the artist. Though the dismal battle over high- and pop-cultural standards rumbles away in the background, popular film-makers and writers have frequently set the cultural pace in the last thirty years. I have treated *GoodFellas* as a generic film because to me genre is a potentially fruitful and creative principle, not a stockpile of hackneyed formulae. It can be said of Scorsese, as it has been of the crime writer Elmore Leonard, that he doesn't 'transcend' the genre. He makes it seem infinite.

# bibliography

# general film

Altman, Rick, *Film Genre*, BFI, 1999
Detailed exploration of the concept of film genre

Bordwell, David, *Narration in the Fiction Film*, Routledge, 1985
A detailed study of narrative theory and structures

– – –, Staiger, Janet & Thompson, Kristin, *The Classical Hollywood Cinema: Film Style & Mode of Production to 1960*, Routledge, 1985; pbk 1995
An authoritative study of cinema as institution, it covers film style and production

– – – & Thompson, Kristin, *Film Art*, McGraw-Hill, 4th edn, 1993
An introduction to film aesthetics for the nonspecialist

Branson, Gill & Stafford, Roy, *The Media Student's Book*, Routledge, 2nd edn 1999

Buckland, Warren, *Teach Yourself Film Studies*, Hodder & Stoughton, 1998
Very accessible, it gives an overview of key areas in film studies

Cook, Pam & Bernink, Mieke (eds), *The Cinema Book*, BFI, 2nd edn 1999

Corrigan, Tim, *A Short Guide To Writing About Film*, HarperCollins, 1994
What it says: a practical guide for students

Dyer, Richard (with Paul McDonald), *Stars*, BFI, 2nd edn 1998
A good introduction to the star system

Easthope, Antony, *Classical Film Theory*, Longman, 1993
A clear overview of writing about film theory

Hayward, Susan, *Key Concepts in Cinema Studies*, Routledge, 1996

Hill, John & Gibson, Pamela Church (eds), *The Oxford Guide to Film Studies*, Oxford University Press, 1998
Wide-ranging standard guide

Lapsley, Robert & Westlake, Michael, *Film Theory: An Introduction*, Manchester University Press, 1994

Maltby, Richard & Craven, Ian, *Hollywood Cinema*, Blackwell, 1995
A comprehensive work on the Hollywood industry and its products

Mulvey, Laura, 'Visual Pleasure and Narrative Cinema' (1974), in *Visual and Other Pleasures*, Indiana University Press, Bloomington, 1989
The classic analysis of 'the look' and 'the male gaze' in Hollywood cinema. Also available in numerous other edited collections

Nelmes, Jill (ed.), *Introduction to Film Studies*, Routledge, 2nd edn 1999
Deals with several national cinemas and key concepts in film study

Nowell-Smith, Geoffrey (ed.), *The Oxford History of World Cinema*, Oxford University Press, 1996
Hugely detailed and wide-ranging with many features on 'stars'

**Thomson, David, *A Biographical Dictionary of the Cinema*,**
Secker & Warburg, 1975
> Unashamedly driven by personal taste, but often stimulating

**Truffaut, François, *Hitchcock*,**
Simon & Schuster, 1966,
rev. edn. Touchstone, 1985
> Landmark extended interview

**Turner, Graeme, *Film as Social Practice*,**
3rd edn, Routledge, 1999
> Chapter four, 'Film Narrative', discusses structuralist theories of narrative

**Wollen, Peter, *Signs and Meaning in the Cinema*,**
BFI 1997 (revised edn)
> An important study in semiology

Readers should also explore the many relevant websites and journals. *Film Education* and *Sight and Sound* are standard reading.

Valuable websites include:

The Internet Movie Database at
www.uk.imdb.com

Screensite at
www.tcf.ua.edu/screensite/contents.html

The Media and Communications Site at the University of Aberystwyth at
www.aber.ac.uk/~dgc/welcome.html

There are obviously many other university and studio websites which are worth exploring in relation to film studies.

# goodfellas

**Bliss, Michael, *Martin Scorsese & Michael Cimino*,** The Scarecrow Press, 1985
> A detailed but critically pedestrian work on the two directors

**Bookbinder, Robert, *Classic Gangster Films*,** Citadel Press, 1993
> An informal survey of earlier titles in the genre, with credits and plot résumés

**Biskind, Peter, *Easy Riders, Raging Bulls*,** Bloomsbury, 1998
> A look at New Hollywood, mixing a detailed account of its working practices with anecdotes and gossip

**Bruzzi, Stella, 'Style And The Hood',** *Sight & Sound*, November 1995
> A two-page article on style, dress and appearance in American and French gangster films

**– – – *Undressing Cinema*,** Routledge, 1997
> Bruzzi's book-length elaboration of her argument, with some perceptive commentary on *GoodFellas*

**Cawelti, John G., 'Chinatown And Generic Transformation In Recent American Films',** in G. Mast & M. Cohen (eds), *Film Theory And Criticism*, OUP 2nd edn, 1979

**Christie, Ian, 'Martin Scorsese's Testament',** *Sight & Sound*, January 1996
> An interview with Scorsese mainly but not wholly addressed to *Casino*.

**Corrigan, Timothy, *A Cinema Without Walls*,** Routledge, 1991

DeCurtis – Kolker

A discursive reading of how New Hollywood and new technology have impacted on American films and their audiences

**DeCurtis, Anthony, 'Martin Scorsese',** *Rolling Stone*, 1 November, 1990

An interview following the US release of *GoodFellas*, with some discussion of his earlier films

**Dougan, Andy, *Martin Scorsese: The Making Of His Movies*,** Orion, 1997

An informative biographical account, plus short film-by-film summaries and an appendix of *Variety* reviews

**– – – *Untouchable Robert De Niro*,** Virgin, rev. edn, 2000

A generally admiring biography of the actor and his relationship with Scorsese

**Friedman, Lawrence. S, *The Cinema Of Martin Scorsese*,** Roundhouse, 1999

Chapter 9 evaluates *GoodFellas* and *Casino* as 'valedictories to the Mob'

**Griffith, Richard, 'Cycles & Genres'** in Bill Nichols (ed.), *Movie & Methods*, University of California Press, 1976 (originally published 1949)

Assesses the first gangster cycle as 'a mirror to subterranean discontent with the American social structure'

**Hardy, Phil (ed.), *Gangsters*,** Aurum, 1998

A decade-by-decade survey, with credits and a brief critical appraisal for each movie, plus a useful introduction

**Hickenlooper, George, *Reel Conversations*,** Citadel Press, 1991

'Means of Redemption', an interview with Scorsese, appears among others with 'foremost directors and critics'

**Hillier, Jim, *The New Hollywood*,** Studio Vista, 1992

A thoughtful introduction to changes in the industry and their consequences

**Jacobs, Diane, *Hollywood Renaissance*,** A.S. Barnes/Tantivy, 1977

Addresses the nature of 'New Hollywood' and its crop of directing talent in the 1970s

**Kefauver, Estes, *Crime In America*,** Gollancz, 1952

A first-person digest by the senator of the hearings and conclusions of the Special Committee to Investigate Crime in Interstate Commerce

**Kelly, Mary Pat, *Martin Scorsese: A Journey*,** Secker & Warburg, 1992

The section on *GoodFellas* includes testimony and opinion from the screenwriters, the producers and the cast

**Keyser, Les, *Martin Scorsese*,** Twayne Publishers, 1992

In the Twayne Filmmakers Series which views the wiseguys in *GoodFellas* as 'unwashed yuppies from hell'

**Kolker, Robert, *A Cinema Of Loneliness*,** 3rd edition, OUP, 2000

Chapter 3, 'Expressions Of The Streets', includes a perceptive, formally inflected analysis of *GoodFellas*

**Kooistra, Paul, *Criminals As Heroes*,** Bowling Green State U.P., 1989

Some reflections on the popular attraction of the criminal, with a stress on the Robin Hood archetype

**Lacey, Robert, *Little Man*,** Century, 1991

A sober, full-dress historical biography of a leading mobster, Meyer Lansky, placed in the context of national organised crime

**Maltby, Richard & Craven, Ian, *Hollywood Cinema*,** Blackwell, 1995

A comprehensive work on the Hollywood industry and its products

**Martin, Richard, *Mean Streets & Raging Bulls*,** The Scarecrow Press, 1997

Subtitled 'The Legacy of Film Noir in American Cinema', it identifies the noir input in early Scorsese pictures

**McArthur, Colin, *Underworld USA*,** Secker & Warburg, 1972

Still one of the most lucid and penetrating short treatments of the crime/gangster picture

**John McCarty, *Hollywood Gangland*,** St Martin's Press, 1993

A brisk and lively survey of 'the movies' love affair with the mob' from pre-generic times

**Mottram, James, *Public Enemies: The Gangster Movie A–Z*,** Batsford, 1998

Basically a checklist of 200 gangster films, with thumbnail reviews and a chronology

**Munby, Jonathan, *Public Enemies, Public Heroes*,** University of Chicago Press, 1999

A historically based analysis of gangster movies from *Little Caesar* to *Touch Of Evil*, emphasising the importance of sound to the new genre

**Murphy, Kathleen, 'Made Men',** *Film Comment*, September/October 1990

A review of *GoodFellas* prefacing the Gavin Smith interview

**Pileggi, Nicholas, *Wiseguy*,** Corgi, 1987

The source text, edited testimony from – principally – Henry and Karen, set in a framing narrative by Pileggi

**Scorsese, Martin & Pileggi, Nicholas, *GoodFellas: The Complete Screenplay*,** Faber, 1990

The published screenplay, described as 'the final continuity script prepared by Thelma Schoonmaker, ACE'

**Smith, Gavin, interview with Martin Scorsese,** in *Film Comment*, September/October 1990

A wide-ranging interview with the director in the wake of *GoodFellas'* US release

**Stephens, Michael, *Gangster Films*,** McFarland & Company, 1996

An alphabetical reference encyclopaedia of the genre

**Stern, Lesley, *The Scorsese Connection*,** BFI, 1995

An imaginative and subjective tracing of intertextual links between Scorsese's movies and others, annoyingly without an index

**Thompson, David & Christie, Ian (eds), *Scorsese on Scorsese*,** Faber 1996

Interviews with an articulate and co-operative Scorsese, and a full filmography to 1995

Thompson – Yaquinto

**Thompson, David, 'Death's Cabbie',** *Sight & Sound*, December 1999

Primarily a piece on *Bringing Out The Dead*, with a stress on the religious undercurrent in Scorsese's films

**Warshow, Robert, 'The Gangster As Tragic Hero',** in The *Immediate Experience*, Atheneum, 1975 (originally published 1958)

A seminal essay treating the movie gangster as a modern American archetype

**Winokur, Mark, 'Eating Children is Wrong',** *Sight & Sound*, November 1991

Reflections on the role of the ethnic family in a number of Mob movies

**Yaquinto, Marilyn, *Pump 'Em Full of Lead*,** Twayne Publishers, 1998

Chapter 10 deals with *GoodFellas* under the heading 'New Age Dons & Wise Guys'

# cinematic terms

**aesthetic** aesthetics is the branch of philosophy which concerns the theory and practice of art, or the beautiful

**auteurisme** the 'authorship theory' of cinema, giving priority to the role of the director, whose personal style and vision are deemed to be the key factor

**charismatic** from 'charisma' – personal magnetism, the quality of inspired and inspiring leaders. Also applied to stars with a strong screen presence

**cinema vérité** a style of film-making that tries to achieve an effect of realism and spontaneity by techniques such as the use of hand-held cameras and minimal editing of sound and image

**classic Hollywood** the mainstream American film industry and its products as it existed from approximately 1930–1960. See studio system

**connotations** in semiotics, the wider associations of a word or image, as opposed to 'denotation', the plain, literal meaning. 'Heart' *denotes* an organ of circulation; it *connotes* love, passion, morale, etc

**dénouement** 'unravelling' – the disentangling of narrative strands in a work of fiction to provide a final resolution

**diegetic** from 'diegesis', meaning 'narrative'. Whatever is diegetic belongs *within* the narrative of a film. Superimposed music is **non-diegetic.** The back story is **pre-diegetic**

**eclectic** 'multiply sourced' – an eclectic work will draw on a variety of styles and ideas

**existential** a complex philosophical term, but in discussions of literature and film it commonly refers to the hero's efforts to bring meaning into an absurd world, or win freedom from the constraints of society, by personal choice and decisive, often extreme, action

**film noir** a group of films made mostly in the 1940s in the US and Europe which were 'dark' both in theme and visual style. They were usually shot in black and white

**freeze-frame** an effect similar to a still photograph, achieved by printing a single frame a number of times in succession

**iconography** the expressive pictorial motifs characteristically associated with a movie genre

**intertextuality** a relationship between two or more artworks that allows them to be read meaningfully in terms of one another

**jump cut** in film, an abrupt as opposed to a smooth transition, compressing time and/or space

**meta-cinema** 'cinema about cinema', i.e. films that refer to their own filmic construction, or to other movies, through the devices associated with modernist or postmodernist cultural strategies

**montage** either just 'editing', or more commonly the rapid and forceful 'impact editing' first theorised by the Soviet film-maker Sergei Eisenstein

**néo-noir** 'noir' refers to film noir – see above. These films are now seen as a major influence on contemporary films with similar dark and 'tough' thematics which, although usually shot in colour, have a similar visual style

**New Hollywood** the American film

# cinematic terms

industry as it has developed from the late 1960s, following the break-up of the old studio system

**otherness** or 'alterity'. The perceived difference that allows outgroups to be stigmatised and stereotyped

**polysemic** 'having many meanings'. Cinema is an information-rich visual medium, in which meanings are multiple and subject to various 'readings'

**preview** the preview system evolved in Hollywood as a way of test-marketing films. New movies were exhibited before general release to gauge the reaction of audiences, who filled in preview cards

**Propp** Vladimir Propp, in his *Morphology of the Folk Tale* (1928), identified a sequence of 'narrative functions' common to a sample of traditional Russian tales. Propp's method has subsequently been adapted to study narrative in modern and contemporary texts

**reception** reception studies, a growing concern of writers on film, consider how audiences 'receive' films, what meanings and impressions they take from them

**semidocumentary** a style that mimics the techniques of documentary (such as location shooting, a 'rough' or spontaneous look, improvised dialogue) to enhance the realism of feature films

**semiotic** semiotics (or semiology) is the study of signs. In cinema the principal sign is the image (or 'iconic sign'). Analytically, the sign is divisible into the 'signifier' – the image itself – and the 'signified' – what it means

**specific form** the element that distinguishes a particular medium – in the case of cinema, moving photographic images

**studio system** classic Hollywood operated from a base of eight major studios: the 'Big Five' (MGM, Warner Bros, Paramount, Twentieth Century Fox, RKO) and the 'Little Three' (Columbia, Universal-International, United Artists)

**vertically integrated** vertical integration meant that big studios owned the means of production, distribution and exhibition of films. Federal action under anti-trust laws, started before the Second World War and completed after it, dismantled the studios' vertically integrated structure

**WASP** acronym for 'White Anglo-Saxon Protestant', historically the earliest settlers and dominant social group in America

# credits

## production company
Warner Bros

## director
Martin Scorsese

## producer
Irwin Winkler

## screenplay
Martin Scorsese &
Nicholas Pileggi

## cinematographer
Michael Ballhaus

## film editor
Thelma Schoonmaker

## production designer
Kristi Zea

## cast
Henry Hill – Ray Liotta

Jimmy Conway – Robert De Niro

Tommy DeVito – Joe Pesci

Paulie Cicero – Paul Sorvino

Karen Hill – Lorraine Bracco

Tuddy Cicero – Frank DiLeo

Frankie Carbone – Frank Sivero

Billy Batts – Frank Vincent

Morris Kessler – Chuck Low

Frenchy – Mike Starr

Sonny Bunz – Tony Darrow

Janice – Gina Mastrogiacomo

Sandy – Debi Mazar

Tommy's Mother – Catherine Scorsese

Vinnie – Charles Scorsese

Young Henry – Chris Serrone

## songs
Tony Bennett, 'Rags To Riches'

Hoagy Carmichael, 'Stardust'

The Crystals, 'Then He Kissed Me'

Al Jolson, 'Toot Toot Tootsie Goodbye'

Tony Bennett, 'The Boulevard Of Broken Dreams'

The Rolling Stones, 'Gimme Shelter'

Sid Vicious, 'My Way'

(Mentioned in the text. For a complete list of the more than forty numbers used, see *GoodFellas: The Complete Screenplay*.)